Cambridge
Collections

Exits and entrances

a drama collection from stage and screen

Edited by John O'Connor
Series editor: Michael Marland

CAMBRIDGE
UNIVERSITY PRESS

CAMBRIDGE UNIVERSITY PRESS

Cambridge, New York, Melbourne, Madrid, Cape Town, Singapore, São Paulo, Delhi

Cambridge University Press
The Edinburgh Building, Cambridge CB2 8RU, UK

www.cambridge.org
Information on this title: www.cambridge.org/9780521730853

First published 2008

Printed in the United Kingdom at the University Press, Cambridge

A catalogue record for this publication is available from the British Library

ISBN 978-0-521-73085-3 paperback

Cover image: Adrian Lester as Hamlet © Pascal Victor / ArtComArt
Cover design by Smith

Contents

General introduction

Acting is something most of us do even before we can properly read or write. We chat with imaginary friends, play games in role with real friends and fill the playground with a thousand mini-plays about true and fictitious events that excite, frighten or amuse us. It seems that drama is in our genes. Perhaps it all started in prehistoric times when our cave ancestors acted out 'the kill' before embarking on a day's hunting. It was certainly extremely important to earlier civilisations such as the Ancient Greeks and Romans, who built imposing theatres and held their dramatists in great respect.

Today drama is to be found everywhere we look: not just on stages of various kinds, but also on cinema, television and computer screens. It can take the form of a play, a sketch or an improvisation, and is a central part of many popular musicals and of opera. It is even essential to many television advertisements, where families discuss cornflakes over the breakfast table and ever-friendly bank managers offer generous loans.

The extracts in this book have been taken from a variety of periods, and are written by authors from a number of different countries and cultures. They include a range of genres, from the lightest comedy to the most serious drama; and feature material from the stage, the cinema and television.

The book is divided into four sections:

- *Identity* contains extracts from plays in which people are forced to think about their position in the world, asking who they are and what they want out of life; while those around them have to learn to accept each individual for what he or she is.
- *Turning points* is about those moments in our lives when we have to make a really important decision, one that will affect our future.
- *Deception* features examples of the numerous plays through the ages in which one character deceives another, whether for fun or with some more serious motive.
- *Laughter* is just that: a collection of comic extracts designed to make you laugh and to appreciate that comedy comes in many forms and has different purposes.

In each section the more challenging extracts come towards the end.

To help you, less familiar words and phrases have been explained at the foot of the pages where they occur. There are suggestions for further reading after each text, and you can find out more about the authors at the end of the book.

You will also find activities throughout the collection, all designed to get you thinking both before and after reading.

Whatever else you do as you read each extract, remember that plays are written in order to be performed. We can learn something from reading a play and talking about it; but we will never fully understand it until we have acted it ourselves, or seen it acted by others – and that is true whether we are talking about *Doctor Who* or Shakespeare.

I hope you enjoy these extracts and that they inspire you to write your own plays, watch other people's and take part yourself in as many as you can.

John O'Connor

1 Identity

When we watch a play we begin to understand a little bit more about what it is to be a human being. We learn about the different ways in which people behave with one another and, in particular, we see that every person has his or her own identity, something that makes them unique and special.

All of the main characters in this section are trying to understand more about themselves, how they relate to the people around them and how they fit in to the society in which they live.

Activities

1   Who are you? What makes up your own identity? Draw a spider diagram with you in the middle. On the outside add details about yourself. You could include, for example:
    ● people and places important to you
    ● your interests
    ● your ambitions
    ● your fears.

2   Think about experiences you have had when you felt out of place. It might have been when you joined a group in which everybody else knew each other, or where you were the only person to disagree with a generally held opinion. Write a paragraph describing how you felt in that situation, and what happened.

3   In pairs, devise a role play in which somebody has to stand up for themselves. Perhaps they have been wrongly accused of something or are being forced to do something they know is wrong. Decide on the characters and situation first, so that you are clear about who you are, what the problem is and what has happened so far.

Doctor Who: Human Nature

by Paul Cornell

This is the opening of an episode of the long-running television series, *Doctor Who*.

The central console[1] of the TARDIS[2] is sparking crazily as MARTHA and THE DOCTOR start to pick themselves up off the floor. THE DOCTOR dashes to MARTHA, grabs her hand and pulls her up, then pulls her eye to eye.

THE DOCTOR	*(urgently)* Did they see you?
MARTHA	I don't know!
THE DOCTOR	Did they see you?
MARTHA	I don't know, I was too busy running!
THE DOCTOR	Martha, it's important – did they see your face?
MARTHA	No, they couldn't have!
	THE DOCTOR runs round the console and starts playing with controls.
THE DOCTOR	Off we go!
	MARTHA comes to stand next to him as he watches the time rotor intently. As a warning beep cuts in, we see symbols on the console screen.
THE DOCTOR	*(annoyed)* Ahhh!
	THE DOCTOR grabs the console screen and reads it.
THE DOCTOR	They're following us.
	He goes back to the controls.

---

[1]**console**   unit holding the main controls
[2]**Tardis**   the Doctor's time-travelling ship

MARTHA   How can they do that? You've got a time machine.

THE DOCTOR   Stolen technology, they've got a Time Agent's vortex manipulator. They can follow us wherever we go, right across the universe – *(pause)* they're never going to stop.

He runs a hand through his hair nervously and stares; then an idea comes to him.

THE DOCTOR   *(quietly)* Unless . . . I'll have to do it . . .

He stares into MARTHA's eyes.

THE DOCTOR   Martha, you trust me don't you?

MARTHA   Of course I do.

THE DOCTOR   'Cause it all depends on you.

He dives below the console to retrieve something, MARTHA watches on in confusion.

MARTHA   What does, what am I supposed to do?

THE DOCTOR reappears holding an ornate pocket watch aloft.

THE DOCTOR   Take this watch, 'cause my life depends on it. The watch, Martha – The watch is –

THE DOCTOR is lying in a bed sporting a pair of blue striped pyjamas. His eyes flick open suddenly, cutting in from the last scene. He blinks in confusion a few times, and we see he is in an ornate Victorian room, wood panelling and framed paintings. After a couple of seconds, he pushes himself to sit up, feet on the floor. As he rubs his eyes, we hear a knock. Shortly after, there is the sound of a door opening.

THE DOCTOR   *(calls)* Come in.

MARTHA enters, wearing a Victorian maid's uniform and carrying a tray of breakfast. As she sees THE DOCTOR sitting on his bed, her eyes widen and she turns back.

MARTHA	Pardon me, Mr Smith, you're not dressed yet. I can come back later –

She turns to go as THE DOCTOR stands, pulling and tying a dressing gown around himself.

THE DOCTOR	No, it's alright, it's alright. Put it down.

MARTHA walks to a table in the middle of the room and sets the tray down, keeping her eyes lowered. THE DOCTOR watches her thoughtfully.

THE DOCTOR	I was, um . . . *(pause)* Sorry, sorry. *(thoughtfully)* Sometimes I have these extraordinary dreams.

MARTHA crosses to the window and pulls the curtains open.

MARTHA	What about, sir?

THE DOCTOR	I dream I'm this . . . *(he searches for the right term)* Adventurer. This . . . daredevil, a madman. 'The Doctor', I'm called. And last night I dreamt that you were there, as my . . . companion.

MARTHA crosses back to the tray on the table – THE DOCTOR's eyes have been following her across the room.

MARTHA	A teacher and a housemaid, sir? That's impossible.

THE DOCTOR	Ah no, a man from another world, though . . .

MARTHA	Well it can't be true because there's no such thing.

THE DOCTOR has moved to the fireplace and looks at the mantel – where the watch is sitting.

THE DOCTOR	This thing . . . *(he picks up the watch)* The watch . . .

MARTHA watches him, hopeful; but after holding it for a second he replaces it on the mantel with a sigh.

THE DOCTOR   Ah, it's funny how dreams slip away. *(He turns back to MARTHA)* But I do remember one thing; it all took place in the future. In the year of Our Lord two thousand and seven.

MARTHA   I can prove that wrong for you sir, here's the morning paper. *(She hands it to him)* It's Monday, November tenth, nineteen thirteen, and you're completely human, sir. *(She smiles at him)* As human as they come.

THE DOCTOR   Mmm, that's me; completely human.

He smiles.

The Union Jack flag is being raised to full mast as a choir of boys sing a hymn. We see an impressive old school building, almost like a fortress, and a group of schoolboys, marching in regimented lines into the school grounds. An early motor car beeps its horn as it drives past the gates to pull up near to the main door. THE DOCTOR, in a suit, mortar board[3] and teacher's gown, walks past a group of students before turning into the main door.

BOY 1   Morning, Sir.

He passes a young boy in the corridor.

BOY   Morning, Sir.

A bell rings, calling the start of school. Further into the building, THE DOCTOR passes more teachers and nods to one who is heading for a flight of stairs.

THE DOCTOR   Headmaster.

A little later, and we see THE DOCTOR taking a history lesson, cane in one hand and textbook in another. The neat copperplate[4] writing on the chalkboard reads

---

[3]**mortar board**   an old-fashioned hat that teachers wore, with a flat top and tassle

[4]**copperplate**   neat handwriting style

'Battle of Waterloo, 18th June 1815'. THE DOCTOR is reading aloud from the textbook while the class look on attentively.

THE DOCTOR   – impediment. The French were all but spent, with only two battalions of the old guard remaining. A final reserve force was charged with protecting Napoleon. By evening, the advance of the Allied troops had forced them to retreat.

Out in the school corridor, MARTHA and JENNY, another maid, are on their hands and knees scrubbing the tiled floor. THE DOCTOR walks past, making MARTHA smile. Her eyes follow him as he passes.

MARTHA   Morning, Sir.

THE DOCTOR slows down a little and answers distractedly.

THE DOCTOR   Yes, hi.

He disappears up the stairs.

JENNY   Head in the clouds, that one. Don't know why you're so sweet on him.

She smiles slyly then they both carry on scrubbing.

MARTHA   He's just kind to me, that's all. Not everyone's that considerate, what with me being –

She points to her face – we assume she means the colour of her skin. JENNY smiles.

JENNY   A Londoner?

MARTHA   Exactly. *(She grins)* Good old London town!

Two senior boys, BAINES and HUTCHINSON walk over the area MARTHA and JENNY are cleaning, and look back as the girls laugh.

BAINES   *(authoritatively)* Ah, now then, you two.

MARTHA and JENNY stop laughing and look up.

BAINES   You're not paid to have fun, are you. Put a little backbone into it.

JENNY   Yes Sir, sorry, Sir.

HUTCHINSON   *(looking at MARTHA)* You there, what's your name again?

MARTHA   Martha, Sir. Martha Jones.

HUTCHINSON   Tell me then, Jones. With hands like those, how can you tell when something's clean?

The two boys laugh cruelly and leave. MARTHA and JENNY watch them.

MARTHA   *(deadpan)* That's very funny, Sir.

JENNY   Careful now, don't answer back.

MARTHA   I'd answer back with my bucket over his head.

JENNY laughs as they both go back to scrubbing.

JENNY	Oh I wish!

JENNY thinks of something and stops, looking after the two boys.

JENNY	Just think though. In a few years' time boys like that will be running the country.
MARTHA	*(quieter)* Nineteen thirteen. They might not.

In one of the upper corridors, MATRON JOAN REDFERN passes a student.

BOY	Excuse me, ma'am.

THE DOCTOR is overloaded with a stack of books as MATRON JOAN REDFERN approaches.

JOAN	Oh, good morning, Mr Smith.

THE DOCTOR fumbles with the top book and it falls to the floor. He quickly steps on it to stop it falling away.

THE DOCTOR	There we go.
JOAN	Let me help you.
THE DOCTOR	No, no, I've got it, no . . . *(He wonders how he is going to pick the book up with his arms full)* Um . . . ah . . . Just to . . . retrieve . . . ah . . . If you could take these – *(he hands her the stack of books, then bends to pick up the book)*
JOAN	Good. *(She smiles warmly)*
THE DOCTOR	No harm done. *(He smiles back at her)* So, um, how was Jenkins?
JOAN	Oh just a cold, nothing serious. I think he's missing his mother, more than anything.
THE DOCTOR	*(sympathetically)* Aw, can't have that.

JOAN   He received a letter this morning so he's a lot more chipper. *(She looks down at the stack of books she is still holding)* I appear to be holding your books.

THE DOCTOR is still staring at MATRON JOAN REDFERN's face, then suddenly snaps back to life.

THE DOCTOR   Yes, so you are! Sorry, sorry.

He starts to relieve MATRON JOAN REDFERN of the books awkwardly.

THE DOCTOR   Just let me –

JOAN   No, why don't I take half?

THE DOCTOR   Ah, brilliant idea, brilliant. Perfect. Division of labour.

JOAN   We make quite a team.

THE DOCTOR   Don't we just.

He is still all smiles, daft in the presence of MATRON JOAN REDFERN.

JOAN   So, these books. Were they being taken in any particular direction?

THE DOCTOR   Yes. Um . . . *(He looks up the corridor, thinking – then turns to the other direction)* This way.

Ever the gentleman, he lets MATRON JOAN REDFERN lead on. In another corridor, he has finally settled into a coherent conversation.

THE DOCTOR   I always say, Matron, give the boys a good head of steam, they'll soon wear themselves out.

JOAN   Truth be told, when it's just you and me, I'd much rather you call me Nurse Redfern. 'Matron' sounds rather . . . well, matronly.

THE DOCTOR   Ah, Nurse Redfern it is then.

JOAN   Though we've known each other all of two
                months, you could even say 'Joan'.

THE DOCTOR   Joan?

JOAN   That's my name.

THE DOCTOR   *(flustered)* Well, obviously.

JOAN   And it's John, isn't it?

THE DOCTOR   Yes, yes it is.

                *A wooden noticeboard is on one wall of the landing –
                MATRON JOAN REDFERN spots a particular notice and
                heads towards it.*

JOAN   Have you seen this, John? The annual dance
                at the village hall tomorrow. It's nothing
                formal, but rather fun by all accounts.
                (hopefully) Do you think you'll go?

                *THE DOCTOR stammers for a moment, unsure how to
                answer.*

THE DOCTOR   *(flustered)* I hadn't thought about it.

JOAN   It's been ages since I've been to a dance, only
                no-one's asked me. *(she laughs nervously – there is a
                short tense silence)*

THE DOCTOR   *(trying to rescue the conversation)* Well, I should ima-
                gine that you would be . . . um . . . I mean I never
                thought you'd be one for . . . I mean there's no
                reason why you shouldn't – if you do, you may
                not . . . I probably won't, but even if I did then I
                couldn't . . . um, I mean I wouldn't want to –

JOAN   The stairs.

THE DOCTOR   It – what about the stairs?

JOAN   They're right behind you.

THE DOCTOR turns to see and overbalances, falling backwards down the stairs and sending the books flying. JOAN turns away for a split second, but we see her concern.

A little later, JOAN is cleaning a cut on the back of THE DOCTOR's head. He groans against the pain.

JOAN   *(hiding a smile)* Stop it. I get boys causing less fuss than this.

THE DOCTOR   *(sulkily)* Because it hurts!

MARTHA bursts in, all concern.

MARTHA   Is he alright?

JOAN   Excuse me, Martha. It's hardly good form to enter a master's study without knocking.

MARTHA   *(a little annoyed)* Sorry, right, yeah. *(she runs back to the door and knocks on it before returning)* But is he alright? *(she looks at THE DOCTOR)* They said you fell down the stairs, Sir.

THE DOCTOR   *(mumbled)* No, it was just a tumble, that's all.

MARTHA   *(to JOAN)* Have you checked for concussion?

JOAN   I have. And I daresay I know a lot more about it than you.

MARTHA remembers her place and nods.

MARTHA   Sorry. I'll just . . . *(she looks at THE DOCTOR and moves towards the desk)* Tidy your things.

THE DOCTOR   I was just telling Nurse Redfern – Matron, um, about my dreams. They are quite remarkable tales.

MARTHA looks up in interest as THE DOCTOR explains to MATRON JOAN REDFERN.

THE DOCTOR	I keep imagining that I'm someone else, and that I'm hiding –
JOAN	Hiding? In what way?
THE DOCTOR	Um . . . er . . . almost every night . . . *(he laughs)* This is going to sound silly –
JOAN	Tell me.
THE DOCTOR	I dream, quite often, that I have two hearts.
JOAN	Well then, I can be the judge of that.

Reaching into a battered doctor's bag, she draws out a stethoscope with a smile. MARTHA has been watching, but turns and walks away as MATRON JOAN RED-FERN places the stethoscope against THE DOCTOR's chest. We hear a heartbeat on the left side of his chest, and MARTHA turns to see the result of the right side. There is nothing.

JOAN	I can confirm the diagnosis – just one heart, singular.

MARTHA seems a little disappointed, but THE DOCTOR laughs at his silliness.

THE DOCTOR	I have written down some of these dreams in the form of fiction . . . um . . . not that it would be of any interest . . .
JOAN	I'd be very interested.

THE DOCTOR looks in amazement, and MATRON JOAN REDFERN nods. THE DOCTOR stands and moves to the desk.

THE DOCTOR	Well . . . I've never shown it to anyone before.

He hands her a black leather-bound journal, and she reads the handwritten title on the first page.

JOAN   'Journal of Impossible Things'

She turns the pages, and we see they are covered in both writing and ink pictures – the central console is sketched on the first page, then the monitor screen section, a detailed sketch of a gasmask victim from his earlier encounter with the nanogenes.[5]

JOAN   Just look at these creatures!

She turns the page again to reveal a Dalek in all its inked glory.

JOAN   Such imagination.

THE DOCTOR   Mmm. It's become quite a hobby.

More pages, more sketches and pages of writing. The face of the Moxx[6] *of Balhoon gives way to a sketch of two Autons, then to the face of one of the clockwork robots that had tried to take the brain of Madame de Pompadour.*

JOAN   It's wonderful. And quite an eye for the pretty girls.

In the centre of the next page is a sketch of Rose's face.

THE DOCTOR   Oh no no, she's just an invention. This character, Rose,[7] I call her, Rose.

MARTHA appears in the background, looking at THE DOCTOR.

THE DOCTOR   *(thoughtfully)* Seems to disappear later on . . .

Another page, another sketch; this time of a quartet of Cybermen – and in the top corner on the next page, a small sketch of the TARDIS. As THE DOCTOR explains it, there is a bigger, more detailed sketch further down the page.

---

[5]**nanogenes**   tiny organisms that repair people's bodies
[6]**the Moxx** . . .   characters from the Doctor's earlier adventures
[7]**Rose**   the Doctor's former companion on his travels

THE DOCTOR   Ah, that's the box, the blue box, it's always there. Like a . . . like a magic carpet, this funny little box that transports me to far away places.

JOAN   Like a doorway?

THE DOCTOR   Mmm.

The next page is a mess of writing, but the pictures stand out brightly – the faces THE DOCTOR has had before.

THE DOCTOR   I sometimes think how magical life would be if things like this were true.

JOAN   If only.

THE DOCTOR   It's just a dream. *(he gives a short, quiet laugh)*

Further reading

You can read many more Doctor Who stories in the series of novels published by BBC Books. If you are interested in other time-travellers, you should read *The Time Machine* by H. G. Wells, first published in 1895. One of the best of all time-travel tales is a short story called *A Sound of Thunder* which can be found in an anthology of short stories by Ray Bradbury, *Golden Apples of the Sun,* (Doubleday, 1953). It explores what can happen if someone goes back and changes time.

The Elephant Man

adapted by Christopher De Vore, Eric Bergren and David Lynch

This is an extract from the screenplay of the 1980 film, *The Elephant Man*, based on real events which took place in the 19th century. John Merrick (played in the film by John Hurt) has suffered throughout his life from a disease which has caused him to become so deformed that he has to wear a hood in public. He is rescued from a circus freak-show by a surgeon, Dr Frederick Treves (Anthony Hopkins), who takes him back to his hospital. The nurses are revolted and frightened by Merrick's appearance, so Treves decides to enlist the help of the matron, Mothershead (Wendy Hiller).

Scene 1   Isolation ward landing

Mothershead knocks on the door. Treves opens it, comes out onto the landing and closes the door.

TREVES   Ah, Mothershead. How are you feeling today?

MOTHERSHEAD   *(suspiciously)* Fine.

TREVES   Good. Excellent. Now then, Mrs Mothershead, I want you to come into this room with me. Inside there is a man with a rather . . . unfortunate appearance.

MOTHERSHEAD   I've heard.

TREVES   Yes . . . Well, I want you to clear up a little mess, a breakfast tray was spilt. And bring up another breakfast. When you've done that, you and I shall give the man a bath. But, Mothershead, I'm counting on your many years of experience to get you through this. Above all, do not scream, do not cry out, or in any way show this man that you are frightened of him . . .

MOTHERSHEAD   Sir, you don't have to worry about me. I'm not the sort to cry out. Shall we go in?

TREVES   Yes . . . Yes, let's go in.

Treves opens the door.

Scene 2   Isolation ward

Mothershead goes right to the mess.

TREVES   *(to the Elephant Man, hereafter Merrick)* I would like you to meet Mrs Mothershead – Mrs Mothershead, Mr John Merrick.

Merrick looks up to Mothershead, then averts his eyes. He looks back at her and sees she has no difficulty being in his presence.

MOTHERSHEAD   How do you do?

Scene 3   Isolation ward landing

At the door of Merrick's attic room stand two buckets of very dirty water. We hear footsteps coming upstairs and see a young porter carrying two buckets of clean, steaming water. He puts them down, knocks on the door, and takes the dirty water downstairs. The door opens, Mrs Mothershead picks up the steaming buckets and takes them inside, shutting the door.

Scene 4   Isolation ward

Merrick is seated in a tin bathtub trying to hide his nakedness. Mrs Mothershead pours the water in. She scrubs his back with obvious distaste, but does her job. Months of filth and accumulated excrescence[1] are turning the bath water a murky black. As Mothershead scrubs, Merrick slowly leans forward in the bath, closing his eyes, apparently oblivious to his surroundings. Treves sits beside him.

TREVES   The disease is shocking.

Merrick's eyes flicker.

TREVES   I wonder how far it can go before it . . .

Merrick flinches and pulls away.

---

[1]**excrescence**   growths, things sticking to the skin

MOTHERSHEAD   Sit still. Don't wiggle about like a pup. I won't stand for any foolishness.

Treves leans forward and looks at Merrick. Merrick grows still, his eyes closed, apparently in a reverie.

TREVES   *(voiceover)* It's pretty certain that if he had the disease as a child, he was abandoned. But in that case, he'd have to have had care. The very fact that he's alive bears that out . . .

(cut to Treves) But, where?

Merrick is listening.

MOTHERSHEAD   The workhouse.

TREVES   Yes! The workhouse!

At this word, Merrick begins to babble wildly. Obviously alarmed, he thrashes about in the tub, spilling water onto the floor. Treves, alarmed now himself, attempts to calm Merrick, who, still babbling, tries to rise from the tub. Mothershead clamps a hand on Merrick's left arm. At her touch, he is instantly subdued, at least physically. He sinks back into the tub and begins to weep. Treves and Mothershead are astounded by the tears rolling down Merrick's cheeks. They stand motionless looking down at the agonized, naked elephant man.

TREVES   *(softly)* The workhouse.

Scene 5   Following buckets of dirty water down a hallway

Scene 6   Back entrance – alley

The Young Porter is exiting with great difficulty through a large iron door carrying the two buckets. He sets one of the buckets down, takes the other and splashes it out into the alley. Some thick sludge dribbles from the empty bucket. Unseen by him, the Night Porter is standing just to the side and he now comes forward. The Young Porter seems nervous in his presence.

The Night Porter looks at his spattered shoes, then up to the Young Porter.

NIGHT PORTER   What's all this, then?

YOUNG PORTER   Mr Treves is scrubbing his Elephant Man.

NIGHT PORTER   Elephant Man?

YOUNG PORTER   Yeah . . . I hear it's a real horror – even made
Mothershead scream.

NIGHT PORTER   Fiend of the night, eh? The Elephant Man.
I think I'll have me a look at that.

*Suddenly the Night Porter kicks the other bucket of filthy
water violently, sending it splashing all over the young
Porter.*

NIGHT PORTER   Now, you need the scrubbing, ducks!

*He lets his cigarette drop to the ground, then stamps and
grinds it with his brass-heeled boot, all the while smiling.
Then he turns on his heel and leaves.*

Scene 7   Cut to

Dark clouds rolling through an evening sky.

Scene 8   Attic ward

*Through the high barred window, we see the dark sky. Merrick is on his bed in
his sleeping posture. A dim gaslight burns in the room.*

Scene 9   Close-up of Merrick's head

His breathing is more regular now.

Scene 10   A general ward

Lights are being turned off.

Scene 11   Another ward

Lights go off.

Scene 12   Back entrance

Large iron door is closed.

Scene 13   Hallway

Half the lights go off.

Scene 14   Hallway

Nurses leave for their quarters — half the lights go off.

Scene 15   Second floor hallway

We hear the slow metallic footfalls of the Night Porter's boots.

Scene 16   Close-up of a gas light in a hallway

The leaping flame makes a low roar.

Scene 17   Cut to another hallway

Somewhere a door is opened and the squeak sounds vaguely like the trumpeting of an elephant. We hear again the metallic footfalls of the Night Porter's boots, and he appears. He goes to the narrow stairway marked 'Isolation'.[2] He stops and casually looks about. He takes a swig of his gin, then starts up the stairs.

Scene 18   Attic ward

Merrick as before — the light is very dim. We hear the echoing footfalls of the Night Porter coming up the stairs. Merrick's head immediately comes up from his knees. As it does, a small object falls from where his head rested. He picks it up and puts it in a pocket of his cloak. It is a portrait of a beautiful woman.

Suddenly the door swings open and the Night Porter, bottle in hand, is standing there. He walks into the room and sees Merrick's shape on the bed.

NIGHT PORTER   Here he is, the old fiend of the night, the terror of London. Let's have a look at you. Let's see what makes 'em scream . . .

He turns up the light and sees Merrick clearly. The Night Porter jumps back, awestruck.

---

[2]**Isolation**   a ward where patients are kept away from contact with others

NIGHT PORTER   Cor Blimey!

*Merrick is trembling. The Night Porter, hardly able to
believe his eyes, moves slowly towards Merrick. He is afraid
but as he reaches the bed, Merrick flinches back. The
Night Porter grins, his fear gone now. He is in control.*

NIGHT PORTER   So this is the Elephant Man. I ain't never seen
nothing like you before. What the bleedin'
hell happened to you?

Merrick cowers as far away from the Night Porter as possible.

NIGHT PORTER   Oh . . . dumb, eh?

He takes a big swallow of the gin and smiles.

NIGHT PORTER   Good. I likes people what can keep quiet.

*He offers Merrick his bottle with a swift, almost jabbing
motion. Merrick pulls away from him.*

NIGHT PORTER   Like a drink? Go on . . . Go on, have some. No?
You should try being more sociable, mate.

*He tentatively[3] presses the bottom of the bottle up against the
hanging growth on Merrick's chest. Encouraged, he touches him
with his fingers. Merrick makes a small whimpering sound.*

NIGHT PORTER   *(grinning)* You and I are going to be good
friends, we are. And, I've got lots of friends
who I know would like to meet you. And they
will, mate . . . they will.

*He moves to the door and turns. Close-up of Night
Porter's face.*

NIGHT PORTER   Welcome to London.

*He moves out the door and it closes. In the bed, Merrick
looks at the door with terror as the heavy footfalls of the
Night Porter recede down the stairs.*

---

[3]**tentatively**   slowly and carefully, uncertain what might happen

Scene 19   Whitechapel Road

We see a horse's head in close-up, snorting steam into the chill morning air.
The horse is harnessed to a milk wagon parked in front of the London. Through
the open back of the wagon we see the Milkman, and past him Treves, walking
towards us.

MILKMAN   Here early again, eh Mr Treves? If you don't
mind my saying so, sir, with your early habits,
you'd 'a made a fine milkman.

TREVES   Good morning, Charley. I'll keep that in mind!
Treves walks up the path into the hospital.

Scene 20   Hallway (morning)

Treves, carrying a bowl, crosses the upper hall and starts to the narrow stairway
to the Isolation Ward. Over his shoulder we see him knock twice on the door.
As the door swings open, the camera pushes past him and we see the room. The
lamp is still burning, but Merrick is nowhere to be seen. Treves enters, looking
about for him.

TREVES   Mr Merrick?

There's movement in the corner beside the bed. Merrick
rises slightly from the shadow. The light from the lamp hits
his frightened eyes.

TREVES   . . . Good morning . . . John. I've brought your
breakfast.

Treves is unsettled by the sight of Merrick cowering down
on the floor. Merrick begins to babble. Treves enters the
room, placing the bowl on the table and going to
Merrick.

TREVES   What are you doing down there? Come up
John, come up on the bed. The cold floor is
bad for you. I won't hurt you, come on now . . .

He helps Merrick up onto the bed and goes back to the
table for the bowl.

TREVES   You must eat. We must keep your strength . . .

He has turned back to the bed, but Merrick has slipped to the floor again, still trying to hide himself in the corner.

TREVES   . . . What on earth is the matter with you?

He puts the bowl down again and goes back to Merrick, who seems very upset at leaving his hiding place.

TREVES   Now please, John, you must do as I say. Come up from there.

He starts to help Merrick up, but Merrick just presses himself farther back in the corner, still babbling. There are two raps at the door. Treves goes to it and lets Mothershead in.

MOTHERSHEAD   Good morning, Mr Treves. It'll be his bathtime soon. Has he eaten?

TREVES   Not quite yet, Mrs Mothershead. There seems to be some difficulty this morning.

They both look at the bed. Merrick has almost disappeared under it.

MOTHERSHEAD   Won't come out, eh?

TREVES   No, he's very upset about something.

MOTHERSHEAD   Just being obstinate, sir. I'll handle it.

She goes to Merrick and takes hold of his left wrist.

MOTHERSHEAD   Alright, my son, none of this fuss. Come up from there, this instant.

She starts to force him up from the floor. Merrick is moaning now, still trying to get away.

TREVES   No! Don't pull at him like that. We don't want to frighten him more than he already is.

By this time Mothershead has almost got him back on the bed.

MOTHERSHEAD   Honestly, sir, you must be very firm with this sort. Otherwise they'd lay about on the floor gibbering all day long. All he understands is a good smack.

They help Merrick settle back on the pillow. Merrick is still making desperate, unintelligible sounds.

TREVES   He's had his share of 'smacks', Mothershead. I expect that's what drives him under the bed. We must use patience and understanding with this man.

MOTHERSHEAD   Perhaps you've got the time for that, Mr Treves, I certainly don't. I've got an entire hospital to look after, and you have your real patients. Don't waste your time with him sir, it's like talking to a wall. I don't mean to be harsh, but truthfully what can you do for him? I'll be back later for his bath. And Mr Carr Gomm[4] would like to see you when you have a moment. Good day, sir.

She exits. Treves shuts the door behind her and turns back to the bed.

TREVES   *(to himself)* What good am I to you . . . ?

He goes to the bed and sits down in front of Merrick, angered by his own seeming uselessness in the situation.

TREVES   . . . What is my purpose? . . . It's so important that I understand you. I want to help you, I want to be your doctor . . . *(directly to Merrick)* but I can't help you unless you help me, unless I know what you are feeling. I believe there's something back there, there's something you want to say, but I've got to understand you. Do you understand me?

Merrick hesitates, then starts babbling again.

4Mr Carr Gomm   chief surgeon at the hospital

TREVES   No! You are going to talk to me! We are going to show them! We're going to show them that you're not a wall. We are going to talk! Do you understand? Nod your head if you understand me!

Slowly Merrick nods yes.

TREVES   You do understand me! You understand. Now you're going to say it. I've got to hear how you say things. Now, very slowly, say 'yes'.

Treves carefully mouths the word.

TREVES   'Yes.'

Merrick is still hesitant, from years of fear, but his eyes betray a growing excitement. Slowly, he tries to talk, his voice a tremulous⁵ whisper.

---

⁵**tremulous**   nervous and shaky

MERRICK   Yyyy . . . Yyye . . . yyyess.

TREVES   (grabbing Merrick's arm) Yes John!

Throughout their dialogue, Merrick is still very garbled,
but he no longer babbles. He makes a great effort to speak
slowly, to form words the way Treves forms them, to be
understood.

MERRICK   . . . Yyes

TREVES   Yyyess.

MERRICK   Yyess.

TREVES   That's much better. I could understand that
'yes'.

MERRICK   (pleased) Yes!

TREVES   Very good! Oh yes! Now listen. I'm going to
say some things to you and I want you to
repeat them . . . um . . . I want you to say
them back to me. Do you understand? I'm
going to say some things to you and I want
you to say them back to me. Do you
understand?

MERRICK   Yes.

TREVES   Excellent! Now, say . . . 'Hello'.

MERRICK   Hello . . .

TREVES   My name is . . .

MERRICK   My . . . name is . . .

TREVES   John Merrick.

MERRICK   John . . . Merrick.

TREVES   Say 'Merrick'.

MERRICK   Merrick . . .

TREVES   Say 'Mmmerrick'.

MERRICK   Mmmerrick.

TREVES   Say 'Mmmerrick'.

MERRICK   Mmmerrick.

TREVES   Well, that's alright. I understand you. Now, say the whole thing again. Hello . . .

MERRICK   *(haltingly)* Hello . . . my name is . . . John Merrick.

Further reading

If you want to learn more about this extraordinary true story, you could read Frederick Drimmer's book called *The Elephant Man,* (Putnam, 1985). The screenplay extract that you have just read was based on two books that tell the true story of Joseph (sometimes called John) Merrick. The first was written in 1923 by Sir Frederick Treves, the doctor who helps Merrick in the film, and is called *The Elephant Man and Other Reminiscences* (Cassell, 1923). The second is *The Elephant Man: A Study in Human Dignity*, written by Ashley Montagu and published by E. P. Dutton in 1971.

A Raisin in the Sun
by Lorraine Hansberry

A Raisin in the Sun is set in the home of a poor black family in 1950s Chicago, USA. Mama is a strong woman in her sixties, Beneatha (Bennie) her 20-year-old daughter, and Ruth, Mama's thirty-year-old daughter-in-law, married to her son, Walter.

This extract is taken from the first scene in the play.

(BENEATHA comes in, brushing her hair and looking up to the ceiling, where the sound of a vacuum cleaner has started up.)

BENEATHA	What could be so dirty on that woman's rugs that she has to vacuum them every single day?
RUTH	I wish certain young women 'round here who I could name would take inspiration about certain rugs in a certain apartment I could also mention.
BENEATHA	*(shrugging)* How much cleaning can a house need, for Christ's sakes.
MAMA	*(not liking the Lord's name used thus)* Bennie!
RUTH	Just listen to her – just listen!
BENEATHA	Oh, God!
MAMA	If you use the Lord's name just one more time –
BENEATHA	*(a bit of a whine)* Oh, Mama –
RUTH	Fresh[1] – just fresh as salt, this girl!
BENEATHA	*(drily)* Well – if the salt loses its savor –

---

[1] **fresh**   cheeky

MAMA   Now that will do. I just ain't going to have you 'round here reciting the scriptures in vain – you hear me?

BENEATHA   How did I manage to get on everybody's wrong side by just walking into a room?

RUTH   If you weren't so fresh –

BENEATHA   Ruth, I'm twenty years old.

MAMA   What time you be home from school today?

BENEATHA   Kind of late. *(With enthusiasm.)* Madeline is going to start my guitar lessons today.

(MAMA and RUTH look up with the same expression.)

MAMA   Your *what* kind of lessons?

BENEATHA   Guitar.

RUTH   Oh, Father!

MAMA   How come you done taken it in your mind to learn to play the guitar?

BENEATHA   I just want to, that's all.

MAMA   *(smiling)* Lord, child, don't you know what to do with yourself? How long it going to be before you get tired of this now – like you got tired of that little play-acting group you joined last year? *(Looking at RUTH.)* And what was it the year before that?

RUTH   The horseback-riding club for which she bought that fifty-five-dollar riding habit that's been hanging in the closet ever since!

MAMA   *(to BENEATHA)* Why you got to flit so from one
           thing to another, baby?

BENEATHA   *(sharply)* I just want to learn to play the guitar.
           Is there anything wrong with that?

MAMA   Ain't nobody trying to stop you. I just won-
           ders sometimes why you has to flit so from
           one thing to another all the time. You ain't
           never done nothing with all that camera
           equipment you brought home –

BENEATHA   I don't flit! I – I experiment with different
           forms of expression –

RUTH   Like riding a horse?

BENEATHA   – People have to express themselves one way
           or another.

MAMA   What is it you want to express?

BENEATHA	*(angrily)* Me! *(MAMA and RUTH look at each other and burst into raucous[2] laughter.)* Don't worry – I don't expect you to understand.
MAMA	*(to change the subject)* Who you going out with tomorrow night?
BENEATHA	*(with displeasure)* George Murchison again.
MAMA	*(pleased)* Oh – you getting a little sweet on him?
RUTH	You ask me, this child ain't sweet on nobody but herself – *(Under breath.)* Express herself! *(They laugh.)*
BENEATHA	Oh – I like George all right, Mama. I mean I like him enough to go out with him and stuff but –
RUTH	*(for devilment)* What does *and stuff* mean?
BENEATHA	Mind your own business.
MAMA	Stop picking at her now, Ruth. *(A thoughtful pause, and then a suspicious sudden look at her daughter as she turns in her chair for emphasis.)* What *does* it mean?
BENEATHA	*(wearily)* Oh, I just mean I couldn't ever really be serious about George. He's – he's so shallow.
RUTH	Shallow – what do you mean he's shallow? He's *rich*!
MAMA	Hush, Ruth.
BENEATHA	I know he's rich. He knows he's rich, too.

---

[2]**raucous**   loud and harsh

RUTH   Well – what other qualities a man got to have to satisfy you, little girl?

BENEATHA   You wouldn't even begin to understand. Anybody who married Walter could not possibly understand.

MAMA   *(outraged)* What kind of way is that to talk about your brother?

BENEATHA   Brother is a flip – let's face it.

MAMA   *(to RUTH, helplessly)* What's a flip?

RUTH   *(glad to add kindling)* She's saying he's crazy.

BENEATHA   Not crazy. Brother isn't really crazy yet – he – he's an elaborate neurotic.[3]

MAMA   Hush your mouth!

BENEATHA   As for George. Well. George looks good – he's got a beautiful car and he takes me to nice places and, as my sister-in-law says, he is probably the richest boy I will ever get to know and I even like him sometimes – but if the Youngers are sitting around waiting to see if their little Bennie is going to tie up the family with the Murchisons, they are wasting their time.

RUTH   You mean you wouldn't marry George Murchison if he asked you someday? That pretty, rich thing? Honey, I knew you was odd –

BENEATHA   No I would not marry him if all I felt for him was what I feel now. Besides, George's family wouldn't really like it.

---

[3]**neurotic**   somebody who worries too much

MAMA	Why not?
BENEATHA	Oh, Mama – the Murchisons are honest-to-God-real-*live*-rich colored people, and the only people in the world who are more snobbish than rich white people are rich colored people. I thought everybody knew that. I've met Mrs Murchison. She's a scene!
MAMA	You must not dislike people 'cause they well off, honey.
BENEATHA	Why not? It makes just as much sense as disliking people 'cause they are poor, and lots of people do that.
RUTH	(*a wisdom-of-the-ages manner. To MAMA*) Well, she'll get over some of this –
BENEATHA	Get over it? What are you talking about, Ruth? Listen, I'm going to be a doctor. I'm not worried about who I'm going to marry yet – if I ever get married.
MAMA *and* RUTH	*If!*
MAMA	Now, Bennie –
BENEATHA	Oh I probably will . . . but first I'm going to be a doctor, and George, for one, still thinks that's pretty funny. I couldn't be bothered with that. I am going to be a doctor and everybody around here better understand that!
MAMA	(*kindly*) 'Course you going to be a doctor, honey, God willing.

BENEATHA	*(drily)* God hasn't got a thing to do with it.
MAMA	Beneatha – that just wasn't necessary.
BENEATHA	Well – neither is God. I get sick of hearing about God.
MAMA	Beneatha!
BENEATHA	I mean it! I'm just tired of hearing about God all the time. What has He got to do with any-thing? Does He pay tuition?[4]
MAMA	You 'bout to get your fresh little jaw slapped.
RUTH	That's just what she needs, all right!
BENEATHA	Why? Why can't I say what I want to around here, like everybody else?
MAMA	It don't sound nice for a young girl to say things like that – you wasn't brought up that way. Me and your father went to trouble to get you and Brother to church every Sunday.
BENEATHA	Mama, you don't understand. It's all a matter of ideas, and God is just one idea I don't accept. It's not important. I am not going out and be immoral or commit crimes because I don't believe in God. I don't even think about it. It's just that I get tired of Him getting credit for all the things the human race achieves through its own stubborn effort. There simply is no blasted God – there is only man and it is he who makes miracles! *(MAMA absorbs this speech, studies her daughter and rises slowly and crosses to*

---

[4]**tuition**   fees to go to college

BENEATHA *and slaps her powerfully across the face.*
After, there is only silence and the daughter drops her eyes
from her mother's face, and MAMA *is very tall before her.)*

MAMA   Now – you say after me, in my mother's house
there is still God. *(There is a long pause and*
BENEATHA *stares at the floor wordlessly.* MAMA *repeats*
the phrase with precision and cool emotion.) In my
mother's house there is still God.

BENEATHA   In my mother's house there is still God. *(A long*
pause.)

MAMA   *(walking away from* BENEATHA, *too disturbed for tri-*
umphant posture.⁵ Stopping and turning back to her
daughter.) There are some ideas we ain't going
to have in this house. Not long as I am at the
head of this family.

BENEATHA   Yes, ma'am.

*(*MAMA *walks out of the room.)*

RUTH   *(almost gently, with profound understanding)* You think
you a woman, Bennie – but you still a little
girl. What you did was childish – so you got
treated like a child.

BENEATHA   I see. *(Quietly.)* I also see that everybody thinks
it's all right for Mama to be a tyrant. But all
the tyranny in the world will never put a God
in the heavens! *(She picks up her books and goes out.)*

RUTH   *(goes to* MAMA's *door)* She said she was sorry.

MAMA   *(coming out, going to her plant)* They frightens me,
Ruth. My children.

---

⁵**posture**   attitude

RUTH You got good children, Lena. They just a little off sometimes – but they're good.

MAMA No – there's something come down between me and them that don't let us understand each other and I don't know what it is. One done almost lost his mind thinking 'bout money all the time and the other done commence to talk about things I can't seem to understand in no form or fashion. What is it that's changing, Ruth?

RUTH *(soothingly, older than her years)* Now . . . you taking it all too seriously. You just got strong-willed children and it takes a strong woman like you to keep 'em in hand.

MAMA *(looking at her plant and sprinkling a little water on it)* They spirited all right, my children. Got to admit they got spirit – Bennie and Walter. Like this little old plant that ain't never had enough sunshine or nothing – and look at it . . . *(She has her back to RUTH, who has had to stop ironing and lean against something and put the back of her hand to her forehead.)*

RUTH *(trying to keep MAMA from noticing)* You . . . sure . . . loves that little old thing, don't you? . . .

MAMA Well, I always wanted me a garden like I used to see sometimes at the back of the houses down home. This plant is close as I ever got to having one. *(She looks out of the window as she replaces the plant.)* Lord, ain't nothing as dreary as the view from this window on a dreary day, is there? Why ain't you singing this morning,

Ruth? Sing that 'No Ways Tired'. That song always lifts me up so – *(She turns at last to see that RUTH has slipped quietly into a chair, in a state of semi-consciousness.[6])* Ruth! Ruth honey – what's the matter with you . . . Ruth!

Further reading

There are a number of plays and novels that deal with the experience of poor black families in the United States, including Mildred Taylor's *Roll of Thunder, Hear My Cry* (Dial Press, 1976). This is a children's novel featuring a black family and their fight against racism.

---

[6]**semiconsciousness**   Ruth is pregnant

Death and the King's Horseman
by Wole Soyinka

Death and the King's Horseman is set in Nigeria some time during World War II when parts of Africa were still ruled by the British. The village king has died, and Elesin, his chief horseman, is expected to 'commit death' and accompany his ruler to the afterlife. Elesin's son, Olunde, now a medical student in Britain, is sent news of the king's death, and returns to the village on the very night his father is due to die.

When this extract opens, the people are drumming in preparation for Elesin's death. But Simon Pilkings, the British District Officer, has heard what Elesin plans to do and is determined to stop him. Unaware of Pilkings's plans, Olunde has arrived at the British government building where a ball is being thrown in honour of the visiting British royal prince. He meets Pilkings's wife, Jane, who has dressed up for the ball in Nigerian dress – a costume from a local death cult.

JANE   Who is that?

OLUNDE   *(emerging into the light)* I didn't mean to startle you madam. I am looking for the District Officer.

JANE   Wait a minute . . . don't I know you? Yes, you are Olunde, the young man who . . .

OLUNDE   Mrs Pilkings! How fortunate. I came here to look for your husband.

JANE   Olunde! Let's look at you. What a fine young man you've become. Grand but solemn. Good God, when did you return? Simon never said a word. But you do look well Olunde. Really!

OLUNDE   You are . . . well, you look quite well yourself Mrs Pilkings. From what little I can see of you.

JANE   Oh, this. It's caused quite a stir I assure you, and not all of it very pleasant. You are not shocked I hope?

OLUNDE   Why should I be? But don't you find it rather hot in there? Your skin must find it difficult to breathe.

JANE   Well, it is a little hot I must confess, but it's all in a good cause.

OLUNDE   What cause Mrs Pilkings?

JANE   All this. The ball. And His Highness being here in person and all that.

OLUNDE   *(mildly)* And that is the good cause for which you desecrate an ancestral mask?[1]

JANE   Oh, so you are shocked after all. How disappointing.

OLUNDE   No I am not shocked Mrs Pilkings. You forget that I have now spent four years among your people. I discovered that you have no respect for what you do not understand.

JANE   Oh. So you've returned with a chip on your shoulder. That's a pity Olunde. I am sorry.

(An uncomfortable silence follows.)

I take it then that you did not find your stay in England altogether edifying.[2]

---

[1]**desecrate an ancestral mask**   the mask is sacred to Olunde's ancestors and he considers it offensive to wear it as fancy dress
[2]**edifying**   fulfilling, enriching

OLUNDE I don't say that. I found your people quite
admirable in many ways, their conduct and
courage in this war for instance.

JANE Ah yes the war. Here of course it is all rather
remote. From time to time we have a blackout drill[3] just to remind us that there is a war
on. And the rare convoy passes through on its
way somewhere or on manoeuvres.[4] Mind you
there is the occasional bit of excitement like
that ship that was blown up in the harbour.

OLUNDE Here? Do you mean through enemy action?

JANE Oh no, the war hasn't come that close. The
captain did it himself. I don't quite understand it really. Simon tried to explain. The
ship had to be blown up because it had
become dangerous to the other ships, even to
the city itself. Hundreds of the coastal popu-
lation would have died.

OLUNDE Maybe it was loaded with ammunition and
had caught fire. Or some of those lethal gases
they've been experimenting on.

JANE Something like that. The captain blew himself
up with it. Deliberately. Simon said someone
had to remain on board to light the fuse.

OLUNDE It must have been a very short fuse.

JANE (shrugs) I don't know much about it. Only that
there was no other way to save lives. No time

---

³**black-out drill**   a practice in which all lights are turned off in case of an
air-raid
⁴**on manoeuvres**   practising battle movements

to devise anything else. The captain took the decision and carried it out.

OLUNDE   Yes . . . I quite believe it. I met men like that in England.

JANE   Oh just look at me! Fancy welcoming you back with such morbid[5] news. Stale too. It was at least six months ago.

OLUNDE   I don't find it morbid at all. I find it rather inspiring. It is an affirmative[6] commentary on life.

JANE   What is?

OLUNDE   That captain's self-sacrifice.

JANE   Nonsense. Life should never be thrown deliberately away.

OLUNDE   And the innocent people round the harbour?

JANE   Oh, how does one know? The whole thing was probably exaggerated anyway.

OLUNDE   That was a risk the captain couldn't take. But please Mrs Pilkings, do you think you could find your husband for me? I have to talk to him.

JANE   Simon? Oh. *(As she recollects for the first time the full significance of OLUNDE's presence.)* Simon is . . . there is a little problem in town. He was sent for. But . . . when did you arrive? Does Simon know you're here?

---

[5]**morbid**   depressing, to do with death
[6]**affirmative**   positive, optimistic

OLUNDE   *(suddenly earnest)* I need your help Mrs Pilkings.
I've always found you somewhat more understanding than your husband. Please find him
for me and when you do, you must help me
talk to him.

JANE   I'm afraid I don't quite . . . follow you. Have
you seen my husband already?

OLUNDE   I went to your house. Your houseboy told me
you were here. *(He smiles)* He even told me how
I would recognise you and Mr Pilkings.

JANE   Then you must know what my husband is trying to do for you.

OLUNDE   For me?

JANE   For you. For your people. And to think he
didn't even know you were coming back! But
how do you happen to be here? Only this
evening we were talking about you. We thought
you were still four thousand miles away.

OLUNDE   I was sent a cable.

JANE   A cable? Who did? Simon? The business of
your father didn't begin till tonight.

OLUNDE   A relation sent it weeks ago, and it said nothing
about my father. All it said was, Our King is
dead. But I knew I had to return home at once
so as to bury my father. I understood that.

JANE   Well, thank God you don't have to go
through that agony. Simon is going to stop it.

OLUNDE   That's why I want to see him. He's wasting his
time. And since he has been so helpful to me I

don't want him to incur the enmity of[7] our people. Especially over nothing.

JANE   (sits down open-mouthed) You . . . you Olunde?

OLUNDE   Mrs Pilkings, I came home to bury my father. As soon as I heard the news I booked my passage home. In fact we were fortunate. We travelled in the same convoy as your Prince, so we had excellent protection.

JANE   But you don't think your father is also entitled to whatever protection is available to him?

OLUNDE   How can I make you understand? He *has* protection. No one can undertake what he does tonight without the deepest protection the mind can conceive. What can you offer him in place of his peace of mind, in place of the honour and veneration[8] of his own people? What would you think of your Prince if he had refused to accept the risk of losing his life on this voyage? This . . . showing-the-flag tour of colonial possessions.[9]

JANE   I see. So it isn't just medicine you studied in England.

OLUNDE   Yet another error into which your people fall. You believe that everything which appears to make sense was learnt from you.

---

[7]**incur the enmity of**   make enemies out of
[8]**veneration**   great respect, worship
[9]**showing-the-flag tour of colonial possessions**   tour of countries that are part of the British Empire, to keep their spirits up (during the war)

JANE   Not so fast Olunde. You have learnt to argue I
        can tell that, but I never said you made sense.
        However cleverly you try to put it, it is still a
        barbaric custom. It is even worse – it's feudal![10]
        The king dies and a chieftain must be buried
        with him. How feudalistic can you get!

OLUNDE *(waves his hand towards the background. The PRINCE is
        dancing past again – to a different step – and all the
        guests are bowing and curtseying as he passes)* And this?
        Even in the midst of a devastating war, look
        at that. What name would you give to that?

JANE   Therapy,[11] British style. The preservation of
        sanity in the midst of chaos.

OLUNDE Others would call it decadence.[12] However, it
        doesn't really interest me. You white races
        know how to survive; I've seen proof of that.
        By all logical and natural laws this war should
        end with all the white races wiping out one
        another, wiping out their so-called civilisation
        for all time and reverting to a state of primit-
        ivism the like of which has so far only existed
        in your imagination when you thought of us.
        I thought all that at the beginning. Then I
        slowly realised that your greatest art is the art
        of survival. But at least have the humility to
        let others survive in their own way.

JANE   Through ritual suicide?

---

[10]**feudal**   the custom reminds Jane of the Middle Ages when a local lord
    had total control
[11]**therapy**   she sees the Prince's visit as a means of healing troubled minds
[12]**decadence**   a sign that Britain is in decline

OLUNDE   Is that worse than mass suicide? Mrs Pilkings, what do you call what those young men are sent to do by their generals in this war? Of course you have also mastered the art of calling things by names which don't remotely describe them.

JANE   You talk! You people with your long-winded, roundabout way of making conversation.

OLUNDE   Mrs Pilkings, whatever we do, we never suggest that a thing is the opposite of what it really is. In your newsreels I heard defeats, thorough, murderous defeats described as strategic victories. No wait, it wasn't just on your newsreels. Don't forget I was attached to hospitals all the time. Hordes of your wounded passed through those wards. I spoke to them. I spent long evenings by their bedside while they spoke terrible truths of the realities of that war. I know now how history is made.

JANE   But surely, in a war of this nature, for the morale of the nation you must expect . . .

OLUNDE   That a disaster beyond human reckoning be spoken of as a triumph? No. I mean, is there no mourning in the home of the bereaved[13] that such blasphemy[14] is permitted?

JANE   *(after a moment's pause)* Perhaps I can understand you now. The time we picked for you was not really one for seeing us at our best.

[13]**the bereaved**   people who have lost someone in the war
[14]**blasphemy**   insult to the dead (usually, an insult to religion)

OLUNDE   Don't think it was just the war. Before that
even started I had plenty of time to study
your people. I saw nothing, finally, that gave
you the right to pass judgement on other
peoples and their ways. Nothing at all.

JANE   (*hesitantly*) Was it the . . . colour thing? I know
there is some discrimination.

OLUNDE   Don't make it so simple, Mrs Pilkings. You
make it sound as if when I left, I took nothing
at all with me.

JANE   Yes . . . and to tell the truth, only this evening,
Simon and I agreed that we never really knew
what you left with.

OLUNDE   Neither did I. But I found out over there. I am
grateful to your country for that. And I will
never give it up.

JANE   Olunde, please . . . promise me something.
Whatever you do, don't throw away what you
have started to do. You want to be a doctor. My
husband and I believe you will make an excellent one, sympathetic and competent. Don't let
anything make you throw away your training.

OLUNDE   (*genuinely surprised*) Of course not. What a strange
idea. I intend to return and complete my train-
ing. Once the burial of my father is over.

JANE   Oh, please . . . !

OLUNDE   Listen! Come outside. You can't hear anything
against that music.

JANE   What is it?

OLUNDE   The drums. Can you hear the change? Listen.

(The drums come over, still distant but more distinct. There is a change of rhythm, it rises to a crescendo and then, suddenly, it is cut off. After a silence, a new beat begins, slow and resonant.)

There. It's all over.

JANE   You mean he's . . .

OLUNDE   Yes Mrs Pilkings, my father is dead. His will-power has always been enormous; I know he is dead.

JANE   *(screams)* How can you be so callous! So unfeeling! You announce your father's own death like a surgeon looking down on some strange . . . stranger's body! You're just a savage like all the rest.

AIDE-DE-CAMP   *(rushing out)* Mrs Pilkings. Mrs Pilkings. *(She breaks down, sobbing.)* Are you alright, Mrs Pilkings?

OLUNDE   She'll be alright. *(Turns to go.)*

AIDE-DE-CAMP   Who are you? And who the hell asked your opinion?

OLUNDE   You're quite right, nobody. *(Going.)*

AIDE-DE-CAMP   What the hell! Did you hear me ask you who you were?

OLUNDE   I have business to attend to.

AIDE-DE-CAMP   I'll give you business in a moment you impudent nigger. Answer my question!

OLUNDE   I have a funeral to arrange. Excuse me. *(Going.)*

AIDE-DE-CAMP   I said stop! Orderly!

JANE   No no, don't do that, I'm alright. And for heaven's sake don't act so foolishly. He's a family friend.

AIDE-DE-CAMP   Well he'd better learn to answer civil questions when he's asked them. These natives put a suit on and they get high opinions of themselves.

OLUNDE   Can I go now?

JANE   No no don't go. I must talk to you. I'm sorry about what I said.

OLUNDE   It's nothing Mrs Pilkings. And I'm really anxious to go. I couldn't see my father before, it's forbidden for me, his heir and successor to set eyes on him from the moment of the king's death. But now . . . I would like to touch his body while it is still warm.

JANE   You will. I promise I shan't keep you long. Only, I couldn't possibly let you go like that. Bob, please excuse us.

AIDE-DE-CAMP   If you're sure . . .

JANE   Of course I'm sure. Something happened to upset me just then, but I'm alright now. Really.
(*The AIDE-DE-CAMP goes, somewhat reluctantly.*)

OLUNDE   I mustn't stay long.

JANE   Please, I promise not to keep you. It's just that . . . oh you saw yourself what happens to one in this place. The Resident's man thought he was being helpful, that's the way we all

react. But I can't go in among that crowd just
now and if I stay by myself somebody will
come looking for me. Please, just say something for a few moments and then you can go.
Just so I can recover myself.

OLUNDE   What do you want me to say?

JANE   Your calm acceptance for instance, can you
explain that? It was so unnatural. I don't
understand that at all. I feel a need to understand all I can.

OLUNDE   But you explained it yourself. My medical
training perhaps. I have seen death too often.
And the soldiers who returned from the front,
they died on our hands all the time.

JANE   No. It has to be more than that. I feel it has to
do with the many things we don't really grasp
about your people. At least you can explain.

OLUNDE   All these things are part of it. And anyway, my
father has been dead in my mind for nearly a
month. Ever since I learnt of the King's death.
I've lived with my bereavement so long now that
I cannot think of him alive. On that journey on
the boat, I kept my mind on my duties as the
one who must perform the rites[15] over his body.
I went through it all again and again in my
mind as he himself had taught me. I didn't want
to do anything wrong, something which might
jeopardise[16] the welfare of my people.

---

[15]**rites**   religious ceremonies
[16]**jeopardise**   put at risk

JANE   But he had disowned you. When you left he
         swore publicly you were no longer his son.

OLUNDE   I told you, he was a man of tremendous will.
         Sometimes that's another way of saying stub-
         born. But among our people, you don't dis-
         own a child just like that. Even if I had died
         before him I would still be buried like his
         eldest son. But it's time for me to go.

JANE   Thank you. I feel calmer. Don't let me keep
         you from your duties.

OLUNDE   Goodnight Mrs Pilkings.

JANE   Welcome home. *(She holds out her hand. As he takes
         it footsteps are heard approaching the drive. A short while
         later a woman's sobbing is also heard.)*

PILKINGS *(off)* Keep them here till I get back. *(He strides
         into view, reacts at the sight of OLUNDE but turns to his
         wife.)* Thank goodness you're still here.

JANE   Simon, what happened?

PILKINGS Later Jane, please. Is Bob still here?

JANE   Yes, I think so. I'm sure he must be.

PILKINGS Try and get him out here as quietly as you
         can. Tell him it's urgent.

JANE   Of course. Oh Simon, you remember . . .

PILKINGS Yes yes. I can see who it is. Get Bob out here.
         (She runs off.) At first I thought I was seeing a
         ghost.

OLUNDE   Mr Pilkings, I appreciate what you tried to do.
         I want you to believe that. I can only tell you
         it would have been a terrible calamity if you'd
         succeeded.

PILKINGS *(opens his mouth several times, shuts it)* You . . . said
         what?

OLUNDE   A calamity for us, the entire people.

PILKINGS *(sighs)* I see. Hm.

OLUNDE   And now I must go. I must see him before he
         turns cold.

PILKINGS Oh ah . . . em . . . but this is a shock to see
         you. I mean er thinking all this while you were
         in England and thanking God for that.

OLUNDE   I came on the mail boat. We travelled in the
         Prince's convoy.

PILKINGS Ah yes, a-ah, hm . . . er well . . .

OLUNDE   Goodnight. I can see you are shocked by the
         whole business. But you must know by now
         there are things you cannot understand – or
         help.

PILKINGS Yes. Just a minute. There are armed policemen
         that way and they have instructions to let no
         one pass. I suggest you wait a little. I'll er . . .
         give you an escort.

OLUNDE   That's very kind of you. But do you think it
         could be quickly arranged?

PILKINGS	Of course. In fact, yes, what I'll do is send Bob over with some men to the er . . . place. You can go with them. Here he comes now. Excuse me a minute.
AIDE-DE-CAMP	Anything wrong sir?
PILKINGS	*(takes him to one side)* Listen Bob, that cellar in the disused annexe of the Residency, you know, where the slaves were stored before being taken down to the coast . . .
AIDE-DE-CAMP	Oh yes, we use it as a storeroom for broken furniture.
PILKINGS	But it's still got the bars on it?
AIDE-DE-CAMP	Oh yes, they are quite intact.
PILKINGS	Get the keys please. I'll explain later. And I want a strong guard over the Residency tonight.
AIDE-DE-CAMP	We have that already. The detachment from the coast . . .
PILKINGS	No, I don't want them at the gates of the Residency. I want you to deploy them at the bottom of the hill, a long way from the main hall so they can deal with any situation long before the sound carries to the house.
AIDE-DE-CAMP	Yes of course.
PILKINGS	I don't want His Highness alarmed.
AIDE-DE-CAMP	You think the riot will spread here?

PILKINGS   It's unlikely but I don't want to take a chance. I made them believe I was going to lock the man up in my house, which was what I had planned to do in the first place. They are probably assailing[17] it by now. I took a round-about route here so I don't think there is any danger at all. At least not before dawn. Nobody is to leave the premises of course – the native employees I mean. They'll soon smell something is up and they can't keep their mouths shut.

AIDE-DE-CAMP   I'll give instructions at once.

PILKINGS   I'll take the prisoner down myself. Two policemen will stay with him throughout the night. Inside the cell.

AIDE-DE-CAMP   Right sir. *(Salutes and goes off at the double.)*

PILKINGS   Jane. Bob is coming back in a moment with a detachment. Until he gets back please stay with Olunde. *(He makes an extra warning gesture with his eyes.)*

OLUNDE   Please, Mr Pilkings . . .

PILKINGS   I hate to be stuffy old son, but we have a crisis on our hands. It has to do with your father's affair if you must know. And it happens also at a time when we have His Highness here. I am responsible for security so you'll simply have to do as I say. I hope that's understood. *(Marches off quickly, in the direction from which he made his first appearance.)*

---

[17]**assailing**   attacking

OLUNDE   What's going on? All this can't be just because he failed to stop my father killing himself.

JANE   I honestly don't know. Could it have sparked off a riot?

OLUNDE   No. If he'd succeeded that would be more likely to start the riot. Perhaps there were other factors involved. Was there a chieftaincy dispute?

JANE   None that I know of.

ELESIN   *(an animal bellow from off)* Leave me alone! Is it not enough that you have covered me in shame! White man, take your hand from my body!

(OLUNDE stands frozen on the spot. JANE understanding at last, tries to move him.)

JANE   Let's go in. It's getting chilly out here.

PILKINGS   *(off)* Carry him.

ELESIN   Give me back the name you have taken away from me you ghost from the land of the nameless!

PILKINGS   Carry him! I can't have a disturbance here. Quickly! stuff up his mouth.

JANE   Oh God! Let's go in. Please Olunde. *(OLUNDE does not move.)*

ELESIN   Take your albino's[18] hand from me you . . .

(Sounds of a struggle. His voice chokes as he is gagged.)

OLUNDE   *(quietly)* That was my father's voice.

---

[18]**albino**   person whose skin lacks colouring

JANE   Oh you poor orphan, what have you come home to?

(There is a sudden explosion of rage from off-stage and powerful steps come running up the drive.)

PILKINGS   You bloody fools, after him!

(Immediately ELESIN, in handcuffs, comes pounding in the direction of JANE and OLUNDE, followed some moments afterwards by PILKINGS and the constables. ELESIN confronted by the seeming statue of his son, stops dead. OLUNDE stares above his head into the distance. The constables try to grab him. JANE screams at them.)

JANE   Leave him alone! Simon, tell them to leave him alone.

PILKINGS   All right, stand aside you. *(Shrugs.)* Maybe just as well. It might help to calm him down.

(For several moments they hold the same position. ELESIN moves a few steps forward, almost as if he's still in doubt.)

ELESIN   Olunde? *(He moves his head, inspecting him from side to side.)* Olunde! *(He collapses slowly at OLUNDE's feet.)* Oh son, don't let the sight of your father turn you blind!

OLUNDE   *(he moves for the first time since he heard his voice, brings his head slowly down to look on him)* I have no father, eater of left-overs.

(He walks slowly down the way his father had run. Light fades out on ELESIN, sobbing into the ground.)

Further reading

If you want to learn about the dramatist Wole Soyinka, read *Aké: The Years of Childhood* (Vintage, 1981), the story of the author's life up to the age of 11. Another of Wole Soyinka's plays is *The Lion and the Jewel* (Oxford University Press, 1966). Unlike *Death and the King's Horseman*, it is humorous, and tells the story of a schoolteacher who comes into conflict with the village chief.

Activities

Doctor Who: Human Nature

Before you read

1 How much do you know about Doctor Who? Draw a spider diagram with 'The Doctor' in the centre and details of:
- the Doctor's enemies
- his companions
- his technology
- times and places he has visited
- what is unique about him
- his most exciting exploits.

What's it about?

2 Martha is a key character in this episode. How can we tell that Martha knows what has happened to the Doctor? What is she feeling about the situation they are in? Which particular moments in this extract does she find especially difficult to handle? Use your answers to these questions to write an entry in her diary.

3 This extract opens in the Doctor's time-machine, the TARDIS, but the rest of it takes place in a specific location at a particular time. In pairs discuss what you have learnt about the setting in which the Doctor and Martha are now working. In particular, what does Martha mean by her reply 'Nineteen thirteen. They might not.'?

Thinking about the text

4 A good script or screenplay allows the reader to visualise what is happening. Draw a sequence of storyboard frames to represent the script from pages 2 to 5, up to 'He smiles.'.

5 In other adventures the Doctor is usually a fast-talking man of action with a unique sense of humour. Look at his speeches and behaviour here. Make a list of the Doctor's speeches and actions which help to create the completely different character of a 1913 schoolteacher.

The Elephant Man

Before you read

1 When Dr Treves first meets John Merrick, he assumes that he is 'an imbecile' because he communicates only in grunts and reacts like a frightened animal. In fact, he turns out to be a sensitive man who, after some practice, can express himself well and can read. As a class, discuss the ways in which people are often misjudged by their appearance.

What's it about?

2 Re-read the extract and then in small groups talk about the different attitudes to John Merrick displayed by:
   - Dr Treves
   - Mothershead, the matron
   - the night porter.

3 What do we learn about John Merrick from Scene 4? Write a paragraph expressing his thoughts after Treves and Mothershead leave the room at the end of the scene.

   What does Merrick think about:
   - being bathed by the matron
   - hearing Treves talk about his disease
   - being reminded of his earlier life in the workhouse?

Thinking about the text

4 By the end of this extract, Merrick is learning to speak clearly once again. What is there about Dr Treves that enables him to succeed with Merrick where others might fail? Working in small groups, read Scenes 1, 4, 19 and 20 and then discuss the way Treves behaves with Mothershead, Merrick and Charley, the milkman. Find examples of Treves's:
   - calmness
   - patience
   - friendliness
   - understanding
   - concern to help Merrick.

12158 Identity

A Raisin in the Sun

Before you read

1 As a class, talk about moments in which an argument has arisen between a parent and child (of any age) over a difference of opinion or belief. This might be from your own experience or based on a situation you have read about or seen on television. What caused the argument? How did it end?

What's it about?

2 In groups of three, discuss the two main characters, Mama and Beneatha. What have you learned about them from the way they speak and behave here? By the end of the scene, whose side are you on? Give reasons for sympathising with (a) Mama and (b) Beneatha.

3 In the same groups, act out the first half of the extract, leading up to the point where Mama slaps Beneatha and forces her to say 'In my mother's house there is still God.' Then look back through the dialogue and talk about the stages by which the argument develops. How do we know that a row is brewing? What things have they already disagreed over? Why do you think Mama and Beneatha have drawn apart?

Thinking about the text

4 In pairs, improvise a conversation between Ruth and her husband Walter (Beneatha's brother) later that day. First, discuss what you know about Ruth and Walter.

In your improvisation think about the following questions:
- How does Ruth describe events between Mama and Beneatha?
- How does she recount the part she played herself?
- How should Walter respond to Ruth?
- Does Walter stand up for Beneatha or condemn her?

5 This play is about an African-American family and is set in 1950s Chicago, USA. But its themes – expression of identity, conflicts between parents and children, the ambitions of people to better themselves – are important to families throughout the world at any time.

Write a page of your own version of this play, set in your neighbourhood in recent times, deciding what conflicts the parents and children will have.

Death and the King's Horseman

Before you read

1   In groups, discuss what you know about different cultures' views of the afterlife. For example, what were the Ancient Egyptians' beliefs? What beliefs do different people hold today?

What's it about?

2   To Pilkings, the tradition whereby the king's chief horseman 'commits death' seems so barbaric that he forcibly prevents it. What arguments does Olunde put forward to defend it, and to criticise the British way of life in return?

3   In pairs, re-read the section in which Jane and Olunde talk about the captain who blew himself up with his ship.
    ●   Talk about the differences between Jane's attitude to the Captain's action and Olunde's. What accounts for those differences?
    ●   In what ways is the story of the Captain relevant to the extract as a whole?

Thinking about the text

4   Read the end of the scene in which Olunde is brought face to face with his father.
    ●   How would you describe Olunde's reactions?
    ●   What do you think is going through his mind?
    ●   Why does he not greet his father warmly?

Discuss your ideas in a small group.

5   Imagine that later that night Jane writes a letter to a friend back in England. What would she say about the evening's events? How might she attempt to make sense of her conversation with Olunde and his reaction to his father? What might she write about:
    ●   Olunde's reactions to her costume
    ●   his defence of the tradition of ritual suicide
    ●   his attitudes to the British
    ●   his reaction when he believes his father has died
    ●   her own feelings after she says 'You're just a savage like all the rest.'
    ●   Olunde's behaviour when he sees his father?

Write her letter.

Compare and contrast

1 This section is called 'Identity'. Compare the ways any two charac-
   ters struggle with the following questions:
   - Who am I?
   - Who are my friends?
   - How should I behave with the people around me?
   - What do I want out of life?

2 Draw up a table that shows the different settings in each of these
   plays. Next to each title state:
   - when the play is set
   - where it is set.

   Then write a short essay comparing two or three of the plays.
   Explain how the setting in each case affects the way the characters
   behave.

3 In small groups, discuss which character you would (a) most like
   to be and (b) least like to be. Talk about the reasons for your
   choices.

4 Two of these extracts – *A Raisin in the Sun* and *Death and the King's
   Horseman* – are from plays written for the stage. The other two –
   Doctor Who and *The Elephant Man* – are screenplays written for tele-
   vision and film, respectively.

   Compare one stage script with one of the screenplays and describe
   the differences. Look particularly at the author's directions in your
   chosen scripts and the different purposes they serve.

2 Turning points

Our lives are full of moments when we have to make a decision. Usually it will be a fairly unimportant one, such as whether or not to take a raincoat or have another sandwich. But every now and then we are faced with a decision knowing that the choice we make will have a significant effect on our future. Stories from theatre, film and television are full of such turning points: for example, Macbeth decides to kill the King, or Frodo spares Gollum's life – and their lives suddenly take a very different turn, in some cases for better, in others for worse.

Activities

1 In groups, think about the important decision points in your lives. They might have come when you met somebody new or had to make a choice at school.
   - What did you do?
   - What did you take into account when you made your decision?
   - How did it affect your life afterwards?
   - Did you do the right thing?

2 Write a short scene in which three or four people have to make an important decision but disagree about what to do. For example, they might be:
   - business people
   - war leaders
   - a family.

3 Draw a short cartoon strip that illustrates an important turning point in history. The first few frames could establish the time in history and the general situation; the others could lead up to the decisive moment. Share your drawing with others to see if they can work out which moment you have illustrated.

The Life and Adventures of Nicholas Nickleby

adapted by David Edgar from the novel by Charles Dickens

In 1980 the Royal Shakespeare Company staged a hugely successful stage adaptation of Charles Dickens's *Nicholas Nickleby*. It was in two parts and involved around 40 actors.

You will see that some speeches are spoken by NARRATORS. All of the cast members share these speeches.

Nicholas's father has died, leaving the family very poor. Their rich uncle insists that Nicholas must look for work, and tells him to answer an advertisement for an assistant teacher in a school in Yorkshire. The headmaster, Wackford Squeers, is in London, and Nicholas goes to meet him.

Scene 5

The coffee house of the Saracen's[1] Head. A table, on which WACKFORD SQUEERS is sitting, reading a newspaper. Near him is a little trunk, on which a small boy, BELLING, is sitting. This scene is set up during:

NARRATOR   And so the uncle, and his nephew, took themselves with all convenient speed towards Snow Hill, and Mr Wackford Squeers.

The narration is carried on by WILLIAM, a waiter at the Saracen's Head. TWO MAIDS enter; and stare at MR SQUEERS.

WILLIAM   And in Snow Hill, near to the jail and Smithfield, is the Saracen's Head, and outside the Saracen's Head are two stone heads of Saracens, both fearsome and quite hideously ugly, and inside, on this January afternoon,

---

[1]**Saracens**   Muslims who fought against Christians in the Middle Ages

stood Mr Squeers, whose appearance was not much more prepossessing.[2]

SQUEERS lowers the newspaper. We see him as the TWO MAIDS describe him to each other.

1ST MAID   He's only got one eye.

WILLIAM   While the popular prejudice runs in favour of two.

2ND MAID   And, look, the side of his face is all wrinkled and puckered.

WILLIAM   Which gave him a highly sinister appearance, especially when he smiled.

1ST MAID   And the eye he's got's a very funny colour.

WILLIAM   Which indeed it was, a kind of greenish grey, in shape resembling the fanlight of a street-door, through which Mr Squeers was glaring at a tiny boy, who was sitting on a tiny trunk, in front of him.

Squeers hires Nicholas and collects two new pupils for his school: Dotheboys Hall. They journey together to Yorkshire.

Scene 9

SQUEERS   *(banging)* Well, then. Hey! Door!

From the darkness, SMIKE appears. He is about 19, but bent over with lameness, and dressed in ragged garments which he has long since outgrown. He pulls open the huge door, and the wind howls as SQUEERS strides into the house.

Smike. Where the devil have you been?

---

[2]**prepossessing**   pleasing to look at

SMIKE	Please, sir, I fell asleep.
SQUEERS	You fell awhat?
SMIKE	Please, sir, I fell asleep over the fire.
SQUEERS	Fire? What fire? Where's there a fire?

During the following, SQUEERS, SMIKE, NICHOLAS and the boys with their luggage move round the stage – as if passing along corridors – as the Squeers' servant PHIB brings on a big chair and then a table to centre stage. This is the Squeers' parlour,[3] and PHIB goes out again to bring on a tray of brandy, glasses and water, placing it on the table.

SMIKE	Please, sir, Missus said as I was sitting up, I might be by the fire for a warm . . .
SQUEERS	Your missus is a fool. You'd have been a deuced[4] deal more wakeful in the cold.

From off, we hear the voice of MRS SQUEERS.

MRS SQUEERS	*(off)* Squeers!
SQUEERS	*(calls)* My love!
MRS SQUEERS	Squeers!

By now SQUEERS is in the parlour area, the boys are standing in the corridor with their luggage, and NICHOLAS is between them, not knowing quite what to do.

SQUEERS	*(to SMIKE)* There's boys. The boys, to bed.

SMIKE takes the boys out, leaving their luggage, as MRS SQUEERS enters.

MRS SQUEERS	Oh, drat the thing.
SQUEERS	What's wrong, my dear?

---

[3]**parlour**   living-room
[4]**deuced**   common alternative to 'damned'

MRS SQUEERS	The school spoon. I can't find it.
SQUEERS	Never mind, my love.
MRS SQUEERS	What, never mind? It's brimstone,[5] in the morning.
SQUEERS	Ah, I forgot. *He helps the search.* Yes, certainly, it is.
NICHOLAS	Uh . . . ?
SQUEERS	We purify the boys' bloods now and then, Nickleby.
MRS SQUEERS	*(crossly)* Purify fiddle-sticks. Don't think, young man, that we go to the expense of flour of brimstone and molasses[6] just to purify them; because if you think we carry on the business in that way, you'll find yourself mistaken, and so I tell you plainly. *SQUEERS is not sure this intelligence is quite discreet. Enter PHIB, who tidies round the table, putting things back on the tray.*
SQUEERS	My dear . . . should you . . .
MRS SQUEERS	Nonsense. If the young man comes to be a teacher, let him understand at once that we don't want any foolery about the boys. They have the brimstone and treacle, partly because if they hadn't something or other in the way of medicine they'd always be ailing and giving

---

[5]**brimstone**   a sulphur mixture given with treacle as a daily medicine
[6]**molasses**   treacle

a world of trouble, and partly because it spoils their appetites and comes cheaper than breakfast and dinner. So it does them good and us good at the same time, and that's fair enough, I'm sure.

SQUEERS looking embarrassed. MRS SQUEERS shoots a glance at him.

Now, where's the spoon?

PHIB has picked up the tray.

PHIB   Uh. Ma'am.

MRS SQUEERS   What is it?

PHIB   S'round your neck.

And indeed the spoon is round MRS SQUEERS' neck. She cuffs PHIB lightly for telling her.

MRS SQUEERS   Why did you not say *before*.

PHIB   M'sorry, ma'am.

PHIB picks up the tray, leaving the brandy bottle, and goes out.

Scene 10

Dotheboys Hall. The school bell rings, the lights come up. The parlour chair and table have gone. SQUEERS shouts to NICHOLAS, who wakes.

SQUEERS   Past seven, Nickleby! It's morning come, and well-iced already. Now Nickleby, come, tumble up, will you?

SQUEERS, with his cane, strides on. NICHOLAS jumps up and, pulling on his coat, goes to him. MRS SQUEERS enters, followed by SMIKE, who carries a bowl of brimstone and treacle. SQUEERS and

NICHOLAS arrive at one side of the stage. MRS SQUEERS and SMIKE at the other. Then, through the darkness at the back of the stage, we see, approaching us, THE BOYS of Dotheboys Hall. They are dressed in the ragged remains of what were once school uniforms. They move slowly, through lameness and sullenness[7] and fear. Then they form themselves into a kind of line, and each boy goes to MRS SQUEERS to receive a spoonful of brimstone and treacle.

There. This our shop, Nickleby.

Each boy gives his number, name, age and reason for being at the school before receiving his dose. Clearly, this is an accepted ritual.

TOMKINS   First boy. Tomkins. Nine. A cripple.

COATES   Second boy. Coates. Thirteen. A bastard.

GREYMARSH   Third boy. Greymarsh. Twelve. Another bastard.

JENNINGS   Fourth boy. Jennings. Thirteen. Disfigured.

MOBBS   Fifth boy.

Pause.

Mobbs. Uh – 'leven.

Pause. He doesn't know what's wrong with him. MRS SQUEERS hits him on the side of the head.

MRS SQUEERS Simpleton!

MOBBS   Fifth. Mobbs. Eleven. Sim-pull-ton.

BOLDER   Sixth. Bolder. Fourteen. Orphan.

PITCHER   Seventh. Pitcher. Ten.

---

[7]**sullenness**   sulkiness, silent low spirits

MRS SQUEERS	Yes!
	Pause.
PITCHER	I'm very. Very. Slow.
MRS SQUEERS	Move on. Move *on.*
JACKSON	Eighth. Johnny.
MRS SQUEERS	Johnny?
JACKSON	Jackson. Thirteen. Illegitimate.[8]
COBBEY	Ninth. Cobbey. Fifteen. Cripple.
PETERS	Tenth. Uh – Peters. Seven. Blind.
SPROUTER	Eleventh. Sprouter. Seven. My father killed my mother.
MRS SQUEERS	Yes?
SPROUTER	Sent away.
ROBERTS	Twelfth. Roberts. Ten. There's something wrong – my brain.
	Squeers' young son, WACKFORD, well-dressed and stout, pushes forward the two SNAWLEY boys and BELLING.
SNAWLEY SNR	Robert Arthur Snawley.
MRS SQUEERS	Number!
SNAWLEY SNR	I'm eleven.
MRS SQUEERS	*(twisting SNAWLEY SNR's ear)* Number, is thirteen.
SNAWLEY SNR	Thirteen.

---

[8]**illegitimate**   he has no known father

SNAWLEY JNR   Uh – fourteen-th. Snawley, H. Uh – seven.

BELLING   Fifteen. Anthony Belling. Seven years of age. A classical and modern – moral,[9] education.

MRS SQUEERS wipes her hands on SMIKE. SQUEERS to WACKFORD.

SQUEERS   Thank you, young Wackford. Thank you, son. And what do you say? And what d'you say, to this?

Pause.

BOYS   For what we have received, may the Lord make us truly thankful.

SQUEERS   Amen.

BOYS   Amen.

SQUEERS   That's better. Now, boys, I've been to London, and have returned to my family and you, as strong and well as ever.

Pause. MRS SQUEERS gestures to a boy.

COATES   *(feebly)* Hip hip.

BOYS   *(equally feebly)* Hooray.

COATES   Hip hip.

BOYS   Hooray.

COATES   Hip hip.

BOYS   Hooray.

SQUEERS takes various letters from his pockets and wanders around among the boys as he speaks.

---

[9] **moral**   to do with right and wrong

SQUEERS   I have seen the parents of some boys, and
            they're so glad to hear how their sons are
            doing, that there's no prospect at all of their
            going home, which of course is a very pleasant
            thing to reflect upon for all parties.
            He continues to perambulate.[10]

            But I have had disappointments to contend
            with. Bolder's father, for instance, was two
            pound ten short. Where is Bolder?
            *The boys around BOLDER kick him and he puts up his
            hand. SQUEERS goes to BOLDER.*

            Ah, Bolder. Bolder, if your father thinks that
            because –
            *SQUEERS suddenly notices warts on BOLDER's hand. He
            grabs the boy's arm.*

            What do you call this, sir?

BOLDER   Warts, sir.

SQUEERS   What, sir?

BOLDER   Warts, sir.

SQUEERS   Warts?

BOLDER   I can't help it, sir. They will come . . . It's
            working in the garden does it sir, at least I
            don't know what it is, sir, but it's not my
            fault . . .

SQUEERS   Bolder. You are an incorrigible[11] young
            scoundrel, and as the last thrashing did you

---

[10]*perambulate*   walk round
[11]**incorrigible**   beyond correction

no good, we must see what another will do towards beating it out of you.

BOLDER looks terrified.

La – ter.

He lets BOLDER go and walks on, reading.

Now, let's see . . . A letter for Cobbey. Cobbey?

COBBEY puts his hand up. SQUEERS hardly acknowledges, but walks on.

Oh. Cobbey's grandmother is dead, and his uncle John has took to drinking, which is all the news his sister sends, except eighteen-pence, which will just pay for that broken square of glass. Mobbs!

MOBBS, not sure whether this will be good or bad news, nervously puts up his hand. It is clear it is not good news when SQUEERS walks to him and stands near.

Now, Mobbs' step-mother took to her bed on hearing that he would not eat fat, and has been very ill ever since. She wishes to know by an early post where he expects to go to, if he quarrels with his vittles;[12] and with what feel-ings he could turn up his nose at the cow's liver broth, after his good master had asked a blessing on it. She is disconsolate[13] to find he is discontented, which is sinful and horrid, and hopes Mr Squeers will flog him into a happier state of mind.

Into MOBBS' ear.

---

[12]**vittles**   food
[13]**is disconsolate**   cannot be cheered up

Which – he – will.

Long pause to let this sink in to everyone. Then:

Right, boys. I'd like you all to meet my new assistant, Mr Nickleby. Good morning, Mr Nickleby.

BOYS   Good morning, Mr Nickleby.

NICHOLAS   Good morning.

SQUEERS   Now, this is the first class in English spelling and philosophy, Nickleby. We'll soon get up a Latin one and hand that over to you.

NICHOLAS joins SQUEERS.

Now, then, where's Smallpiece?

BOYS   Please, sir . . .

SQUEERS   Let any boy speak out of turn and I'll have the skin off his back!

He points to JENNINGS.

JENNINGS   Please, sir, he's cleaning the back parlour window.

SQUEERS   So he is, to be sure. We go on the practical mode of teaching, Nickleby; C-l-e-a-n, clean –

BOYS   Clean.

SQUEERS   Verb active, to make bright, to scour. W-i-n, win, –

BOYS   Win –

SQUEERS   D-e-r, der –

BOYS   Der, winder –

SQUEERS   Winder, a casement. When a boy knows this out of a book, he goes and does it. It's just the same principle as the use of the globes.

***

SQUEERS   That's our system, Nickleby. What do you think of it?

NICHOLAS   It's a very useful one, at any rate.

SQUEERS   I believe you. Greymarsh, what's a horse?

GREYMARSH   A beast, sir.

SQUEERS   So it is. A horse is a quadroped,[14] and quadroped's Latin for beast, as anybody that's gone through the grammar knows, or else where's the use in having grammars at all?

NICHOLAS   Where indeed.

SQUEERS   *(to GREYMARSH)* And as you're so perfect in that, go to *my* horse, and rub him down well, or I'll rub *you* down. The rest go and draw water up till somebody tells you to leave, for it's washing day tomorrow, and they'll want the coppers filled.

THE BOYS hurry out, MOBBS and BOLDER hurrying more than the others.

Except – for Mobbs and Bolder.

Everyone stops. Some of THE BOYS push MOBBS and BOLDER forward, towards SQUEERS. Then the others go out, as MRS SQUEERS and WACKFORD go too. SMIKE tries to go as well.

---

[14]**quadroped**   he means 'quadruped': a four-legged animal

Stay there, Smike. They'll need taking to their beds.

He turns to NICHOLAS.

This is the way we do it, Nickleby.

SQUEERS lifts his cane. Blackout. NARRATORS appear in a little light. As they speak this narration, we see NICHOLAS sit morosely[15] down at the side. SQUEERS, SMIKE, MOBBS and BOLDER have gone.

NARRATORS   And Nicholas sat down, so depressed and
                 self-degraded[16] that if death could have
                 come upon him then he would have
                 been happy to meet it.
           The cruelty of which he had been an
                 unwilling witness,
           The coarse and ruffianly behaviour of
                 Squeers,
           The filthy place,
           The sights and sounds about him,
           All contributed to this feeling.
           And when he recollected that, being there as
                 an assistant, he was the aider and
                 abetter[17] of a system which filled him
                 with disgust and indignation,
           He loathed himself.

Blackout.

---

[15]***morosely***   gloomily
[16]**self-degraded**   humiliated, disgraced
[17]**abetter**   accomplice, helper

Scene 13

The common dormitory.[18] *THE BOYS asleep. SMIKE is sitting. NICHOLAS,*
still sitting at the side of the stage, now stands, and goes to SMIKE. NICHOLAS
carries a book.

NICHOLAS   Hello.

SMIKE looks up, scared, and flinches a little.

Please, don't be frightened.

NICHOLAS crouches down near SMIKE. He puts down
his book.

You're shivering.

Pause. NICHOLAS stands to go. He stops when SMIKE
speaks.

SMIKE   Oh, dear.

NICHOLAS turns back.

Oh, dear. Oh, dear. My heart. Will break. It will.

Louder, more forceful.

It *will.* I know it *will.*

NICHOLAS   *(embarrassed, looking round)* Shh, shh.

SMIKE   Remember Dorker, do you?

NICHOLAS   Dorker?

SMIKE   I was with him at the end, he asked for me.
Who will I ask for? Who?

Pause. NICHOLAS doesn't know what SMIKE is talking
about.

NICHOLAS   Who will you ask for when?

SMIKE back into himself again.

---

[18]**common dormitory**   place where Nicholas and all the boys sleep

SMIKE	No One. No Hope. Hope Less.
	Slight pause.
NICHOLAS	*(feebly)* There's always hope.
SMIKE	*(to himself)* Is there?
	SMIKE turns again to NICHOLAS. Forcefully.
	O-U-T-C-A-S-T. A noun. Substantive.[19] Person cast out or rejected. Abject.[20] And forsaken. Homeless. Me.
	NICHOLAS looks at SMIKE. He doesn't know what to say. Pause. Then FANNY (Squeers' daughter) enters, behind NICHOLAS. She takes in the scene.
FANNY	Oh – I'm sorry.
	NICHOLAS turns.
	I was looking for my father.
NICHOLAS	He's not here.
FANNY	I see.
	Pause.
	I beg your pardon, sir. How very awkward.
NICHOLAS	Please, please don't apologise.
FANNY	I thank you, sir. Oh . . . Sir.
	FANNY curtseys, turns, turns back, turns again and goes. NICHOLAS turns to go out too, when he realises he's left his book. He looks back to SMIKE, who has picked up the book and is holding it to himself. NICHOLAS decides to leave SMIKE with the book. SMIKE is left alone, with the sleeping boys.
	Blackout.

---

[19]**substantive** another word for 'noun'
[20]**abject** completely without hope

Nicholas hates the cruel treatment inflicted on the boys, and feels
particularly sorry for Smike.

Scene 18

*The dormitory at Dotheboys Hall. Night. The boys enter and lie down on the bare
stage. SMIKE enters and sits, with Nicholas' book. NICHOLAS enters with a
candle, to see SMIKE trying to read the book. SMIKE can't work out what to do.*

SMIKE   Can't do it. With the book. Can't do it, with
the book, at all.

NICHOLAS   Oh, please. Don't cry.

SMIKE crying.

Don't. For God's sake. I cannot bear it.

SMIKE whimpering

They are more hard on you, I know. But,
please . . .

SMIKE   Except for you, I die.

NICHOLAS   No, no. You'll be better off, I tell you, when
I'm gone.

SMIKE picks it up after a second.

SMIKE   You gone.

NICHOLAS   Shh. Yes.

SMIKE   You going?

NICHOLAS   I was speaking to my thoughts.

SMIKE   *Tell* me. Will you? Will you go?

Pause.

NICHOLAS   I shall be driven to it. Yes. To go away.

Pause.

SMIKE   Please tell me. Is away as bad as here?

Pause.

NICHOLAS   Oh, no. Oh, no, there's nothing –

SMIKE   Can I meet you there? Away?

NICHOLAS   Well, yes . . . you can, of course . . .

SMIKE   Can I meet you there? Away? And I will find
you, in away?

NICHOLAS   You would. And, if you did, I'd try to help
you.

*Pause. NICHOLAS moves away with the candle and sits.
He takes out a paper and a pen. He is writing a letter to
KATE, his sister.*

I miss you terribly, but at least I feel that if my
work here prospers – I miss you terribly.

Pause.

I took a Latin class today. The boys are –
they are not advanced and there is much
to do.

Pause.

The countryside is –

*Pause. He puts away the letter. He blows out the candle.
Darkness.*

Scene 19

*The same. A bell rings offstage, and then cold, morning light. The boys and
NICHOLAS are in the same positions, but, in the blackout, SMIKE has slipped
away.*

SQUEERS   *(off)* Hey! Hey, you up there? Are you going to
sleep all day?

NICHOLAS   We shall be down directly, sir.

He gestures to the boys, who speed up.

SQUEERS   *(off)* Well, you'd better be, or I'll be down on some of you in less – Where's Smike?

NICHOLAS goes to SMIKE's place, but sees he isn't there. The boys are nearly fully up.

(off) I said – where's Smike?

NICHOLAS turns and calls.

NICHOLAS   He isn't here, sir.

SQUEERS   *(off)* What? Not there?

Pause. SQUEERS enters, rushes to SMIKE's place. He sees SMIKE is absent.

What does this mean? Where have you hid him?

NICHOLAS   I have not seen him since last night.

SQUEERS   Oh, no?

Turning to the boys.

And you? You boys? Have any of you –

JENNINGS, who is obscured from SQUEERS by other boys.

JENNINGS   Please, sir . . .

SQUEERS   Yes? What's that?

JENNINGS   Please, sir, I think he's run away.

SQUEERS   Who said that?

BOYS   Jennings, sir.

SQUEERS   And, where is Jennings?

BOYS   Here, sir.

JENNINGS is pushed forward by his fellows. SQUEERS to JENNINGS.

SQUEERS   So you think he's run away, do you?

JENNINGS   Yes, sir. Please, sir.

SQUEERS   And what, sir, what reason have you to suppose that any boy would *want* to run away
from this establishment?

SQUEERS hits JENNINGS on the face.

Eh, sir?

*JENNINGS says nothing. SQUEERS looks to NICHOLAS,
who is looking away. SQUEERS to NICHOLAS.*

And you, Nickleby. I s'pose you think he's run
away?

NICHOLAS   I think it's highly likely, yes.

SQUEERS   You do? Perhaps you *know* he's run away?

NICHOLAS   I do not know, sir. And I'm glad I did not, for
it would then have been my duty to have
warned you.

SQUEERS   Which, no doubt, you would have been
devilish sorry to do.

NICHOLAS   I should indeed, sir.

MRS SQUEERS enters.

MRS SQUEERS   What's going on? Where's Smike?

SQUEERS   He's gone.

MRS SQUEERS   *(an order, to SQUEERS)* Gone? Well, then,
we'll find him, stupid. We must search
the roads. He hasn't any money, any
food. He'll have to beg. He must be on
the public road.

SQUEERS   *(going towards the exit)* That's true.

MRS SQUEERS   *(following)* And when we catch him, oh . . .

SQUEERS turns his back to the boys. Slowly.

SQUEERS   And when we catch him, I will only stop just short of flaying[21] him alive. So, follow your leader, boys, and take your pattern by Smike. If you dare.

The SQUEERSES go out. NICHOLAS and the boys follow.

The runaway Smike is quickly recaptured and brought back to Dotheboys.

Scene 22

The Dotheboys Hall schoolroom. Bare stage. The boys enter, two of them dragging a pair of steps, the thrashing-horse.[22] They put it centre stage. The boys form two lines either side of it.

NICHOLAS enters, and looks in horror at the thrashing-horse. SQUEERS enters, with a long cane.

SQUEERS   Is every boy here? Every boy keep his place.

Pause.

Nickleby, to your place, sir. Coates. Jackson.

COATES and JACKSON go out. NICHOLAS moves near the thrashing-horse. MRS SQUEERS, FANNY, YOUNG WACKFORD and PHIB enter, and stand to one side. COATES and JACKSON re-enter, dragging SMIKE, who is bound, and filthy, clearly having been caught after spending the night rough. He is brought down to the thrashing-horse.

SQUEERS   Untie him, sirs.

The two boys untie SMIKE.

---

[21]**flaying**   skinning
[22]**thrashing-horse**   wooden structure on which boys are placed to be beaten

Now, sir, what do you have to say for yourself?

Pause.

Nothing, I suppose?

Pause. SMIKE glances at NICHOLAS, who is looking away.

Well, then. Let's begin.

SMIKE   Oh, spare me, sir.

SQUEERS   What's that?

SMIKE   Oh, spare me, sir.

SQUEERS   Oh, that's all, is it? Well, I'll flog you within an inch of your life, but I will spare you that.

Pause.

Coates, Jackson.

COATES and JACKSON help SMIKE on to a step of the thrashing-horse. COATES and JACKSON tie SMIKE to the horse.

SMIKE   I was driven to it, sir.

SQUEERS   Driven to it? Not your fault, but mine?

MRS SQUEERS   Hm. That's a good one.

SQUEERS goes a little upstage, turns, runs, and delivers the first blow. SMIKE cries out, SQUEERS grunts. He goes upstage again, runs, and delivers the second blow. He is back upstage again, when NICHOLAS takes a slight step forward.

NICHOLAS   Uh . . . This must stop.

SQUEERS looks round.

SQUEERS   Who said that? Who said stop?

NICHOLAS   I did. I said that it must stop, and stop it will.

Pause.

I have tried to intercede.[23] I have begged for-
giveness for the boy. You have not listened.
You have brought this on yourself.

SQUEERS   *(dismissively, preparing for his next stroke)* Get out.
Get out.

*NICHOLAS walks to stand between SQUEERS and
SMIKE.*

NICHOLAS   No sir. I can't.

SQUEERS   Can't? You can't? We'll see.

*SQUEERS walks to NICHOLAS and strikes his face.
NICHOLAS doesn't respond.*

Now leave, sir, and let me to my work.

*NICHOLAS turns, as if to go, then suddenly turns
back, grabs SQUEERS, pulls him round, and hits
him.*

What?

NICHOLAS   You have –

*SQUEERS tries to hit NICHOLAS, but NICHOLAS
seizes the cane and beats SQUEERS with it. During
the ensuing, the following things happen: MRS
SQUEERS, WACKFORD and eventually FANNY
come to SQUEERS' aid – somewhat ineffectually;[24]
the boys crush round to see, and eventually to obscure,
the fight. And SMIKE, let go, slips away. There is
much shouting.*

MRS SQUEERS   What do you think you're doing, you
madman?

FANNY   Get off him! Get off him, you monster!

---

[23]**intercede**   step in to help somebody in difficulty
[24]**ineffectually**   uselessly, in vain

WACKFORD   Beastly! Beastly, man! You beast!

And NICHOLAS, finished, breaks through the boys and runs out.

MRS SQUEERS   After him! After him, you vermin![25] Move, run after him!

The boys, who have no intention of doing anything of the sort, nonetheless disperse, revealing SQUEERS, sitting on the ground, holding himself.

Oh, Squeery, Squeery.

She helps SQUEERS to his feet.

Oh, my Squeery.

MRS SQUEERS takes SQUEERS out. WACKFORD and FANNY follow.

Scene 25

NICHOLAS on his own in the countryside. Bare stage.

NICHOLAS   It's morning.

NICHOLAS turns to walk out. Something he hears makes him stop. He turns back. SMIKE stands there.

Oh, Smike. Oh – Smike.

NICHOLAS turns quickly to SMIKE, who falls to his knees.

Why do you kneel to me?

SMIKE   To go. Go anywhere. Go everywhere. To the world's end. To the churchyard grave.

Pause.

---

[25]**vermin**   low-life, disgusting creatures like rats and cockroaches

I can. You'll let me. Come away with you.

Pause.

You are my home.

NICHOLAS stands there. He doesn't know what to do. SMIKE turns his face away. He's crying. NICHOLAS puts his hand out to SMIKE. SMIKE looks back. He sees the hand. NICHOLAS helps SMIKE to his feet, and the two of them go slowly out together.

Further reading

The scenes in this play extract were based on Chapters 5–13 of Charles Dickens' novel *Nicholas Nickleby*. If you read on, you can discover what happened to Nicholas and to his sickly companion Smike. There are further descriptions of Victorian school life in other 19th-century novels, such as Charlotte Brontë's *Jane Eyre* and Dickens' *David Copperfield*.

Treasure Island

adapted by David Calcutt from the novel by Robert Louis Stevenson

This play is an adaptation of Robert Louis Stevenson's *Treasure Island*. In David Calcutt's version, Jim Hawkins, now an adult, appears from time to time as a narrator to recall the events of his youth.

The scene at the start of this extract, Act 2 Scene 3, is set in Bristol, some time in the 18th century. The young Jim Hawkins, Squire Trelawney and Doctor Livesey are about to set sail. They have with them a treasure map found in the belongings of a dead pirate, Billy Bones.

Scene 3

CHORUS enter, as SAILORS, brisk, lively, creating the impression of a busy, bustling sea-port.

1ST SAILOR	And he arrives there late next morning . . .
2ND SAILOR	Steps down, still sleepy, from the long night's coach ride . . .
3RD SAILOR	Into the salt-sharp, sea-bright, ocean port . . .
4TH SAILOR	Where tall ships jostle the crowded harbour . . .
5TH SAILOR	Masts sway . . .
6TH SAILOR	Sails slap . . .
1ST SAILOR	Ropes strain at their moorings . . .
2ND SAILOR	Eager to break loose . . .
3RD SAILOR	Leave dry land behind . . .
4TH SAILOR	Sailing for foreign shores, distant horizons . . .
5TH SAILOR	And where the songs of the sailors lift to the breeze . . .

6TH SAILOR   And circle the sun with the wheeling gulls.

(The CHORUS sings a sea-shanty.[1] JIM and HUNTER enter, JIM carrying his bag, and gazing around him in wonder. When the sea-shanty is finished, TRELAWNEY enters to JIM and greets him heartily. We are in the room TRELAWNEY has taken at an inn on the harbour-side.)

TRELAWNEY   Jim! A pleasure to see you again! Good journey? Capital! *(To HUNTER.)* Hunter. Take Jim's bag, stow it on board. *(To JIM.)* You'll go on board yourself later, my boy.

(HUNTER takes JIM's bag and goes. TRELAWNEY continues speaking hurriedly, hardly pausing for breath or allowing any interruption.)

For now, here's your first command. Go to the *Spyglass Inn*. It's just along the harbour. You can't miss it. Introduce yourself to the landlord. He's to be our ship's cook. Capital fellow! A real sea-dog. Lost his leg fighting for King and country and he's eager to take ship again. I met him by chance and it was a fortune that I did. He's assembled the best crew you could find. I think he must know half the seafaring men in Bristol. You tell him that he's to come immediately. For we sail tomorrow, Jim. Tomorrow, with the rising of the sun!

JIM   Did you say he'd lost a leg, sir?

TRELAWNEY   That's right. What of it? Doesn't scare you, does it?

JIM   No, sir . . . only the Captain, when he first came to our inn . . . he warned me to look out for a man with one leg . . . a seafaring man . . .

---

[1]**sea-shanty**   sailors' song, often sung while working

TRELAWNEY   Did he, now? And you think my man and his might be the same?

JIM   I don't know. It just . . . put me in mind of his warning . . .

TRELAWNEY   Then put it clean out of your mind! I'm a fair judge of character, and I say our cook's no more a villain than I am. I'll stake my reputation and my life on it! You get along, now and make your acquaintance with him. You'll see straight away I'm right.

(TRELAWNEY turns from JIM.)

JIM   Squire – you haven't told me the gentleman's name . . .

(SILVER enters, his left leg cut off at the knee, supporting himself with a crutch.)

SILVER	Silver. John Silver. Long John, some call me.

(JIM turns to SILVER. TRELAWNEY goes. We are now at SILVER's inn. The chorus of SAILORS gathers, as if at the inn. Others enter and join them — including TOM MORGAN, GEORGE MERRY, and SILVER's wife, REBECCA. BLACK DOG is also among them.)

	Such is my name, to be sure. And what might yours be?
JIM	My name's Jim, Mr Silver. Jim Hawkins. Squire Trelawney sent me . . .
SILVER	The Squire! Then you must be our cabin-boy. Give me your hand, Jim. *(He shakes JIM's hand.)* Rebecca! Come over here. Meet Jim Hawkins, cabin-boy on the *Hispaniola*. This is my missus, Jim. Rebecca Silver.
JIM	Pleased to meet you, Mrs Silver.
REBECCA	Likewise, Jim.
SILVER	He has some news from the Squire. We have our sailing orders, I'll be bound.
JIM	That's right, Mr Silver. The Squire says you're to come straight away. We sail tomorrow.
SILVER	Tomorrow! And not a day too soon! You'll be looking forward to it, eh? A young lad out on his first sea-voyage. I remember the first time I went to sea. About the same age as you, I was. He's a fine-looking lad, don't you think, Rebecca?
REBECCA	He is, that. The kind of boy we might have been blessed with John, had the powers that be granted it so.

SILVER	The very thought was in my own mind. I wish I was young again, Jim. No more than a lad, like you, and all the world before me.

(During the above, JIM has been looking around at the SAILORS, and his eyes have suddenly fallen upon BLACK DOG. He gives a gasp of recognition. At the same time, BLACK DOG sees JIM.)

JIM	That man . . . !
SILVER	Eh? What is it?
JIM	That man there! It's Black Dog!

(BLACK DOG jumps up.)

REBECCA	I don't care who he is! He's trying to make off without paying his score![2]
SILVER	George! After him!
JIM	Stop him!

(BLACK DOG runs off, pushing his way past several SAILORS, and GEORGE MERRY chases after him.)

REBECCA	What did you say his name was?
JIM	Black Dog – he's a buccaneer – one of those who attacked our inn.
SILVER	The Squire told me of that. One of those swabs,[3] was he. And in my house! Tom Morgan! Was that you drinking with him?

(MORGAN comes across to SILVER.)

MORGAN	Yes, John . . .
SILVER	You never clapped eyes on him before, did you?

---

[2]**score** bill for what he has drunk
[3]**swab** sailor (who does jobs such as 'swabbing', or mopping, the deck)

MORGAN   No, sir. Never.

REBECCA   That's good for. If I knowed you was mixed
up with the like of that scum, you'd never
have put another foot in this house!

SILVER   Get back to your place, for a lubber,[4] Tom
Morgan.

(MORGAN returns to his place.)

REBECCA   He's an honest man, Tom Morgan. Only he's
stupid.

SILVER   Not you, though, Jim. You're a smart lad, I
can see that. Smart as paint. Tell me that
swab's name again?

JIM   Black Dog.

SILVER   Black Dog. I don't know the name. Do you,
Rebecca?

REBECCA   No. But now I come to think of it, I do recall
seeing him in here before – only once or
twice. And both times he was with a blind
beggar . . .

JIM   Yes! That was another of them! Blind Pew!

REBECCA   Pew. Aye, that was his name. He looked a
shark, he did, John. And to think the two of
them were here, drinking our rum, and we
never knowed what they was.

(GEORGE MERRY enters.)

MERRY   I lost him, John.

---

[4]**lubber**   fool

SILVER   Lost him, did you, George! That's bad. And him never having paid his score, neither!

REBECCA   It's a bad business all round. There's only one thing for it, John. You and the boy here had best go straight away and tell the Squire all about it.

SILVER   You're right, Rebecca. Dooty is dooty, and the Squire must be told. Even though it might be he thinks twice about having me aboard, now, knowing I keep such bad company.

(SQUIRE TRELAWNEY and DOCTOR LIVESEY enter to JIM and SILVER. REBECCA, the chorus of SAILORS go. We have now returned to TRELAWNEY's room.)

TRELAWNEY   Nonsense! I won't hear of it! You weren't to know who the scoundrel was. And it shows an honest heart that you came and told us of it straight away.

SILVER   I'm mighty relieved to hear you say that, sir. For the sake of my honour and trust more than anything.

TRELAWNEY   Your honour's beyond doubt, Silver! And you have our complete trust. Isn't that so, Livesey?

LIVESEY   Indeed he does.

SILVER   Thank you very much, gentlemen. I am greatly obliged to you. I'll take my leave of you, now. You have business to attend to, and so do I. *(To JIM.)* I'll see you later, boy, once we're aboard.

(SILVER turns and makes his way off. TRELAWNEY calls after him.)

TRELAWNEY   All hands aboard by four this afternoon.

(SILVER turns and salutes TRELAWNEY with great ceremony.)

SILVER   Aye, aye, sir.

(He grins, then turns and goes. TRELAWNEY turns to LIVESEY and JIM.)

TRELAWNEY   What did I tell you? The man's a perfect card![5]

LIVESEY   I have to say, Trelawney, I agree with you. You have made a good choice there. John Silver certainly suits me.

Scene 4

HUNTER enters. During this scene, JIM moves away to sit a little apart. He takes a piece of rope, and practises tying a ship's knot, constantly failing, and trying again.

HUNTER   Begging your pardon, Squire . . .

TRELAWNEY   Yes, Hunter. What is it?

HUNTER   Captain Smollett is here, sir. He wishes to speak with you.

TRELAWNEY   Show him in, then.

HUNTER   Very good, sir.

(HUNTER goes. TRELAWNEY turns to JIM.)

TRELAWNEY   I wonder what he wants. He's an able man, by all accounts, but stiff, Livesey. Stiff! There's something in him that makes me bristle.

(CAPTAIN SMOLLETT enters.)

---

[5]**card**   entertaining character

TRELAWNEY	Captain Smollett! All's well I hope? Everything shipshape and seaworthy?
SMOLLETT	I'll speak to you plain, sir, and what I have to say is this. I don't like this voyage and I don't like the men.
TRELAWNEY	Don't you, indeed! And perhaps you don't like the ship, either!
SMOLLETT	She seems a good enough craft . . .
TRELAWNEY	Or your employer, eh? Perhaps you don't like him . . . ! *(LIVESEY cuts in.)*
LIVESEY	Captain. You have either said too much or not enough. You say you don't like this voyage? Now, why?
SMOLLETT	When I was engaged, I was given to understand that neither I nor any of the crew were to know our destination until we had set sail. So far so good. I've sailed under sealed orders[6] before. But now I find that every man before the mast[7] knows more than I do!
LIVESEY	Indeed? And what do they know?
SMOLLETT	That we're sailing for treasure – and that you have a map of our destination. And what's more, the very latitude and longitude of it are common knowledge!

---

[6]**sealed orders**   instructions not to be opened until the ship has put to sea
[7]**every man before the mast**   all the ordinary sailors

LIVESEY	Trelawney. How do you explain this?
TRELAWNEY	I can't!
LIVESEY	We all swore to keep the matter secret!
TRELAWNEY	I never breathed a word of it, Livesey!
LIVESEY	Then who did? Perhaps it was me, or Jim, here, or Hunter . . .
SMOLLETT	It doesn't much matter who it was. What matters is, the secret's out. And what are we to do about it?
LIVESEY	What do you suggest, Captain?
SMOLLETT	Going after treasure's a troublesome business. But, if you are determined to proceed with this voyage . . .
TRELAWNEY	We are.
SMOLLETT	Then I feel it only wise to take certain precautions.
LIVESEY	Which are?
SMOLLETT	First, whoever has this map in his possession, let him keep it to himself, and let no more be spoken of it, or of treasure, among the men. There's been too much loose talk already.
LIVESEY	(Looking at TRELAWNEY.) Indeed there has. And next?
SMOLLETT	The powder and arms. They're being stored in the forehold.[8] I suggest it might be better to

---

[8] **forehold**   below-deck storage area at the front of the ship

store them in the hold beneath your own cabin. And give all your own people berths⁹ in the same quarter.

LIVESEY   So that the stern of the ship becomes a garrison,¹⁰ with all weapons to hand.

SMOLLETT   You have my drift exactly, Doctor.

LIVESEY   And then if trouble does arise . . .

SMOLLETT   Not that I believe it will. If I did I wouldn't set sail. But I am the ship's captain, and responsible for the life of every man aboard of her. I'd be failing in my duty if I didn't ensure that every precaution against trouble had been taken.

LIVESEY   And so it shall be, Captain Smollett, just as you say. You can rest assured of that. Can't he, Trelawney?

TRELAWNEY   *(Sullenly.)* Yes.

SMOLLETT   Very good. In that case, I'll take my leave of you and go aboard. Gentlemen.

(SMOLLETT goes.)

TRELAWNEY   That man is intolerable! Did you hear him, Livesey? He more or less accused me of loose talk! Me! His employer! I've half a mind to go after him and . . .

LIVESEY   You'll do no such thing. The man talked sense. The most sense I've heard since this

---

⁹**berths**   places to sleep
¹⁰**garrison**   military post

enterprise was begun. And you're to be congratulated for it.

TRELAWNEY   What?

LIVESEY   Contrary to all my notions, I believe you've managed to get two honest men aboard – that man, and John Silver!

(TRELAWNEY and LIVESEY go, leaving JIM alone still working at tying the knot.)

Scene 5

ADULT JIM narrates.

ADULT JIM   A troublesome business. A dangerous business. But how little I knew it, then. How little I knew of the human soul, and what gold can do to it. For what lay ahead was no voyage of childish adventure, no innocent isle of treasure. It was a country of betrayals, bloodshed and horror, filled with the darkness of the human heart.

(SILVER enters.)

SILVER   What's all this talk of darkness? Horror and bloodshed? Those are no thoughts to fill a lad's head with. It's the light we're sailing into, Jim. The golden light of the sun, burning high and bright in a hot blue sky! Light in our eyes and laughter in our hearts, and a life filled up with joy to overflowing. That's the treasure we're after.

(JIM has succeeded in tying the knot. He shows it to SILVER.)

JIM   Done it! Look!

SILVER   A sheepshank![11] Couldn't've tied one better
          myself. You're smart, Jim. Smart as paint. I
          knew it the minute I clapped eyes on you. And
          we'll have you a regular seafaring man before
          we're out of harbour!

          *SILVER claps his arm round JIM's shoulders, and the two
          of them make their way up on to a raised area. ADULT
          JIM remains below.*

ADULT JIM   So he wooed me with his words, spun a web
            of fine gold about me, as we stood on deck
            in the dawn light, watching the sun clear the
            far horizon, and the ship sprang to life about
            me, and I caught my breath in the sharp salt
            wind.

            *(Chorus of SAILORS enters, with GEORGE MERRY,
            ISRAEL HANDS, REDCAP, TOM MORGAN, CAPTAIN
            SMOLLETT, LIVESEY, TRELAWNEY, and HUNTER.
            Also another sailor, DICK. All SAILORS create the
            impression of a ship. CHORUS and others narrate.)*

1ST SAILOR   Dawn comes and the night's work's done.

MERRY   Everything stowed, fastened, battened.

2ND SAILOR   The ship's company piped aboard.[12]

REDCAP   Farewells made, orders given.

SMOLLETT   All hands on deck! Jump to it man!

3RD SAILOR   And our moorings are loosed[13] and the
             anchor's weighed![14]

---

[11]**sheepshank**   a kind of sailor's knot
[12]**piped aboard**   a whistle would be blown to announce that everyone was
      on board
[13]**moorings are loosed**   ropes between the ship and the dock are untied
[14]**weighed**   raised

HANDS	Tip us a stave,[15] Barbecue!
SILVER	That I will, Israel!

(SILVER sings out the verse of the shanty, as some of the SAILORS mime turning the capstan.[16])

SILVER	Fifteen men on a dead man's chest
ALL	Yo! Ho! Ho! And a bottle of rum!
SILVER	Drink and the devil had done for the rest.
ALL	Yo! Ho! Ho! And a bottle of rum!
SILVER	We hit a storm in 'forty-seven
ALL	Yo! Ho! Ho! And a bottle of rum!
SILVER	And many a man was sent to heaven
ALL	Yo! Ho! Ho! And a bottle of rum!
SILVER	The rope, the rum and the Yellow Jack
ALL	Yo! Ho! Ho! And a bottle of rum!
SILVER	Delivered the rest to hell and back.
ALL	Yo! Ho! Ho! And a bottle of rum!
SILVER	But one man of her crew alive
ALL	Yo! Ho! Ho! And a bottle of rum!
SILVER	That put to sea with seventy-five
ALL	Yo! Ho! Ho! And a bottle of rum!

(JOHN stops singing. The men cheer.)

---

[15]**tip us a stave**   sing us a song (sailors' slang)
[16]**capstan**   the huge cylinder around which the ship's cable is wound; it is turned to raise the anchor

4TH SAILOR	The anchor's a-weigh, and the ship casts free . . .
MORGAN	Loose of her moorings, out from the harbour . . .
DICK	And the land slips away and we turn to the south . . .
5TH SAILOR	As we hoist the sails . . .
HANDS	And they fill with the wind . . .
6TH SAILOR	And it drives us onward across the world.

Scene 6

TRELAWNEY, LIVESEY, HUNTER and SMOLLETT go. SAILORS and the rest go about their duties. SILVER stands next to JIM and they gaze outwards together.

SILVER	There's nothing like, Jim. Casting off from land, with a full wind in your sails. The sky above you and the waves beneath, and nothing but a few planks of timber and sheets of canvas between you and eternity. It makes my heart sing, it does. It sounds the very depths of me. The sea's a great mystery, lad, a mystery that calls to every one of us born. And who can fathom it, eh? Not I, though I've sailed it these forty years.
	(He pats JIM on the shoulder, and goes. JIM remains, looking out to sea. ADULT JIM narrates from below.)
ADULT JIM	There's little to tell of the journey. I was set to work, helping Silver in the galley.[17] And unwearyingly kind to me, he was, and patient, with always a cheering word or a tale of his times at sea. And I saw, too, how respected he

---

[17]**galley**   the ship's kitchen

was by the rest of the men, how in all things they deferred[18] to him, as if he was their true captain.

(HANDS speaks to JIM.)

HANDS   He's no common man, is Long John. He had good schooling in his younger days, and can speak like a book when he's minded.

MERRY   And brave, too. A lion's nothing alongside of Barbecue.

JIM   Why do you call him Barbecue?

HANDS   He's ship's cook, isn't he? There's no man alive more skilled than he at skewering fresh meat on the end of a spike.

(MORGAN, MERRY and REDCAP all laugh at this. SILVER has entered. He speaks sharply to them.)

SILVER   That's enough of that idle talk, Israel Hands! Be about your duties. And the rest of you. Or it'll be nothing but ship's biscuits[19] you'll get to crack your teeth on. *(To JIM.)* You come along with me, now, Jim. There's work to be done, if these lubbers are going to have anything to fill their bellies.

(SILVER and JIM go. ADULT JIM narrates as CAPTAIN SMOLLETT, TRELAWNEY and LIVESEY enter.)

ADULT JIM   On the whole, it was a happy voyage, and every man on board well content – except for the Captain and the Squire. The Squire made no bones about the matter – he despised the

---

[18]**deferred**   gave way
[19]**ship's biscuits**   very hard and dry basic food for sailors

Captain. And the Captain, on his part, remained stiff and distant, and never spoke, but when spoken to.

TRELAWNEY   Well, Captain. What have you to say about the men now? A fine crew, are they not?

SMOLLETT   I'll own[20] I seem to have been wrong about them. There's some of them as brisk as I'd like to see.

TRELAWNEY   And the ship?

SMOLLETT   She's a good ship.

(TRELAWNEY turns to LIVESEY.)

TRELAWNEY   There, Livesey . . .

SMOLLETT   But we haven't reached our destination. And we're not home yet. And I say again, I don't like this voyage!

(SMOLLETT turns briskly from TRELAWNEY and goes. TRELAWNEY speaks in a fury.)

TRELAWNEY   Confound the man, Livesey! A trifle more of him and I shall explode!

(TRELAWNEY marches off, angrily. SILVER enters with JIM. JIM is carrying a large stone bottle. SILVER speaks to LIVESEY.)

SILVER   Begging your pardon, Doctor. It's grog[21] time for the men, and I was wondering if you might be partial to a cup yourself.

LIVESEY   Very decent of you, Silver. Yes, I will take a little.

---

[20]**own**   admit
[21]**grog**   watered-down rum

SILVER   George Merry. Give the good Doctor a cup. Be
sharp about it!

(MERRY gets a cup and gives it to LIVESEY.)

Fill the Doctor's cup for him, Jim, then see to
these others.

LIVESEY   Don't fill it, Jim. Just a little, if you please.

*(JIM pours some of the rum into the DOCTOR's cup,
then fills cups for some of the other men. LIVESEY drinks,
and gasps. SILVER grins.)*

SILVER   What do you say, Doctor? A fine drop of grog,
isn't it?

(LIVESEY speaks, his voice hoarse.)

LIVESEY   Yes, Silver. Very fine indeed.

SILVER   Will you take a drop more?

LIVESEY   No . . . ! No thank you, Silver. One drop will
be . . . quite sufficient . . . thank you.

*(He gives the cup back to MERRY, who drains what
LIVESEY has left. Still reeling from the effects of the rum
LIVESEY goes. SILVER turns to JIM.)*

SILVER   Have you done, Jim?

JIM   Yes, Mr Silver.

SILVER   Let's take a little ease, then. Sit you down alongside me here, and have a yarn with Long John.

*(SILVER and JIM sit together, away from the others. As
they sit, ADULT JIM narrates.)*

ADULT JIM   So we drove on through fair weather, south by
south-west, with a steady breeze and a quiet
sea. And during those warm and sunlit days, it
was my greatest pleasure to be in his company

and listen, entranced, to the many fantastic tales he told.

SILVER   It's a great pity I don't have Cap'n Flint with me on this voyage.

JIM   Captain Flint? The pirate?

SILVER   No, not him. This Cap'n Flint I'm talking of, she's a parrot. I had her with me on most my voyages, before I was dismasted.[22] And I'd've brought her with me on this, only she's too old now.

JIM   How old is she?

SILVER   Two hundred years, maybe. And don't you be surprised at that, for they lives forever, mostly, do those birds. Before I had her, she sailed along the Spanish Main[23] with Captain England,[24] the pirate.

JIM   She must have seen some wickedness in her life, then.

SILVER   She has, Jim, it's true. If anybody's seen more wickedness in the world than that bird, it can only be the Devil himself. She's smelled powder, sure enough. And you should hear her squawk and swear blue fire! *(He imitates a parrot's squawk.) Stand by and go about!*[25] *Hang him from the yard-arm!*[26] *Pieces of eight!*[27] *Pieces of*

---

[22]**was dismasted**   lost my leg
[23]**Spanish Main**   the coasts of the Caribbean Sea
[24]**Captain England**   a famous, real-life pirate
[25]***Stand by and go about!***   Get ready to change course!
[26]***yard-arm***   the mast's cross-piece (from which sailors were hanged)
[27]***Pieces of eight***   Spanish gold coins

eight! That's her favourite, and no wonder, the
ill-gained gold she must've seen in her time.
Pieces of eight!

(JIM and SILVER laugh.)

Two hundred years old, Jim. And she'll be
squawking still, I reckon, when we're all of us
long gone and meat for the worms or the
fishes.

*(He rises, takes up his crutch and goes, leaving JIM sitting
alone. HANDS speaks to JIM.)*

HANDS   Aye. An uncommon man, is Long John. You
stay alongside of him, young Hawkins, and
you'll come to no harm.

*(HANDS turns from JIM and goes. He's followed by
REDCAP, TOM MORGAN, and DICK.)*

Further reading

With the success of films such as the *Pirates of the Caribbean* series,
pirate stories are very popular these days. If you want to read more, try
William Goldman's *The Princess Bride* (which features a character called
'the Dread Pirate Roberts'), and *The Pirates! In an Adventure with
Scientists* by Gideon Defoe (Orion Books, 2004), in which the Pirate
Captain encounters not just his arch enemy Black Bellamy, but also
the famous Charles Darwin.

Trifles

by Susan Glaspell

John Wright has been murdered, found in bed with a rope around his neck. His wife Minnie claims that she found him dead when she woke up, but she has been charged and is now in prison awaiting trial.

George Henderson, the County Attorney (a lawyer whose job it is to prosecute Minnie), has come to the Wrights' house with the Sheriff, Henry Peters. With them is a neighbour, Lewis Hale, who visited the Wrights on the day of the murder, spoke to Minnie and was shown the body. So far they have been able to find nothing incriminating. Neither can they see any possible motive Minnie might have had for killing her husband.

Hale's and Peters's wives have accompanied the men and are now in the Wrights' gloomy and unwelcoming farmhouse kitchen, collecting some items to take to Minnie in prison, while the men inspect the scene of the murder upstairs.

MRS PETERS	*(starting to speak, then in a low voice)* Mr Peters says it looks bad for her. Mr Henderson is awful sarcastic in a speech and he'll make fun of her sayin' she didn't wake up.
MRS HALE	Well, I guess John Wright didn't wake when they was slipping that rope under his neck.
MRS PETERS	No, it's strange. It must have been done awful crafty and still. They say it was such a – funny way to kill a man, rigging it all up like that.
MRS HALE	That's just what Mr Hale said. There was a gun in the house. He says that's what he can't understand.
MRS PETERS	Mr Henderson said coming out that what was needed for the case was a motive; something to show anger, or – sudden feeling.

MRS HALE	*(who is standing by the table)* Well, I don't see any signs of anger around here. *(She puts her hand on the dish towel which lies on the table, and stands looking down at table, one half of which is clean, the other half messy.)* It's wiped to here. *(She makes a move as if to finish work, then turns and looks at loaf of bread outside the bread-box. She drops the towel. Then in that voice of coming back to familiar things.)* Wonder how they are finding things upstairs. I hope she had it a little more tidy up there. *(She moves left.)* You know it seems kind of *sneaking*. Locking her up in town and then coming out here and trying to get her own house to turn against her!
MRS PETERS	But, Mrs Hale, the law is the law. *(She goes centre above table.)*
MRS HALE	*(crossing right)* I s'pose 'tis. *(Unbuttoning her coat.)* Better loosen up your things, Mrs Peters. You won't feel them when you go out.
	MRS PETERS takes off her fur tippet, goes to hang it on hook at back of room left centre, then stands looking at the small corner table up left.
MRS PETERS	*(moving left)* She was piecing a quilt.[1] *(She brings a large sewing-basket from the table up left, and puts it on the table centre, and they look at the bright pieces.)*
MRS HALE	It's a log cabin pattern. Pretty, isn't it? I wonder if she was goin' to quilt it or just knot it?[2]
	Voices have been heard coming down the stairs. The SHERIFF enters, followed by HALE and the COUNTY ATTORNEY.[3]

[1]**piecing a quilt**   sewing together pieces of material to make a patterned bed-cover
[2]**quilt it or just knot it**   two ways of joining the pieces of material together: knotting is much faster than quilting
[3]**County Attorney**   a lawyer in charge of bringing people to trial in one section of an American state

SHERIFF   They wonder if she was going to quilt it or just knot it! *(He crosses up centre and opens the door.)* *The men laugh; the women look abashed.*

COUNTY ATTORNEY   *(rubbing his hands over the fire)* Frank's fire didn't do much up there, did it? Well, let's go out to the barn and get that cleared up.

The men exit centre.

MRS HALE   *(resentfully)* I don't know as there's anything so strange, our takin' up our time with little things while we're waiting for them to get the evidence. *(She sits right of the big table, smoothing out a block[4] with decision.)* I don't see as it's anything to laugh about.

MRS PETERS   *(apologetically)* Of course they've got awful important things on their minds. *(She takes the chair from left of table to above table and sits.)*

MRS HALE   *(examining another block)* Mrs Peters, look at this one. Here, this is the one she was working on, and look at the sewing! All the rest of it has been so nice and even. And look at this! It's all over the place! Why, it looks as if she didn't know what she was about!

After she has said this they look at each other, then start to glance back at the door. After an instant MRS HALE has pulled at a knot and ripped the sewing.

MRS PETERS   Oh, what are you doing, Mrs Hale?

MRS HALE   *(mildly)* Just pulling out a stitch or two that's not sewed very good. *(Threading a needle.)* Bad sewing always made me fidgety.

⁴**block**   piece of fabric for quilting

MRS PETERS   *(nervously)* I don't think we ought to touch things.

MRS HALE   I'll just finish up this end. *(Suddenly stopping and leaning forward.)* Mrs Peters!

MRS PETERS   Yes, Mrs Hale?

MRS HALE   What do you suppose she was so nervous about?

MRS PETERS   Oh – I don't know. I don't know as she was nervous. I sometimes sew awful queer when I'm just tired.

MRS HALE starts to say something, looks at MRS PETERS, then goes on sewing.

Well, I must get these things wrapped up. They may be through sooner than we think. *(Putting apron and other things together.)* I wonder where I can find a piece of paper, and string. *(She rises and crosses to right.)*

MRS HALE   In that cupboard, maybe.

MRS PETERS   *(looking at the cupboard)* Why, here's a birdcage. *(She holds it up.)* Did she have a bird, Mrs Hale? *(She moves back centre.)*

MRS HALE   Why, I don't know whether she did or not – I've not been here for so long. There was a man around last year selling canaries cheap, but I don't know as she took one; maybe she did. She used to sing real pretty herself.

MRS PETERS   *(glancing around)* Seems funny to think of a bird here. But she must have had one, or why would she have a cage? I wonder what happened to it? *(She moves up above the table.)*

MRS HALE   I s'pose maybe the cat got it.

MRS PETERS   No, she didn't have a cat. She's got that feeling some people have about cats – being afraid of them. My cat got in her room and she was real upset and asked me to take it out.

MRS HALE   My sister Bessie was like that. Queer, ain't it?

MRS PETERS   *(examining the cage)* Why, look at this door. It's broke. One hinge is pulled apart.

MRS HALE   *(also looking)* Looks as if someone must have been rough with it.

MRS PETERS   Why, yes. *(She brings the cage forward and puts it on the table.)*

MRS HALE   I wish if they're going to find any evidence they'd be about it. I don't like this place. *(She rises and crosses below table to the fire left.)*

MRS PETERS   But I'm awful glad you came with me, Mrs Hale. It would be lonesome for me sitting here alone. *(She sits above the table.)*

MRS HALE   It would, wouldn't it? But I tell you what I do wish, Mrs Peters. *(Stepping centre.)* I wish I had come over sometimes when *she* was here. I – *(Looking round the room.)* – wish I had.

MRS PETERS   But of course you were awful busy, Mrs. Hale – your house and your children.

MRS HALE   I could've come. I stayed away because it weren't cheerful, and that's why I ought to have come. *(Moving left, then above table to right.)* I – I've never liked this place. Maybe because it's down in a hollow and you don't see the road. I dunno what it is, but it's a lonesome place and always was. I wish I had come over to see Minnie Foster[5] sometimes. I can see now – *(She shakes her head and sits right of the table.)*

MRS PETERS   Well, you mustn't reproach[6] yourself, Mrs Hale. Somehow we just don't see how it is with other folks until something turns up.

MRS HALE   Not having children makes less work – but it makes a quiet house, and Wright out to work all day, and no company when he did come in. Did you know John Wright, Mrs Peters?

MRS PETERS   Not to know him; I've seen him in town. They say he was a good man.

MRS HALE   Yes – good; he didn't drink, and kept his word as well as most, I guess, and paid his debts. But he was a hard man, Mrs Peters. Just to pass the time of day with him – *(She shivers.)* Like a raw wind that gets to the bone. *(She pauses, her eye falling on the cage.)* I should think she would 'a' wanted a bird. But what do you suppose happened to it?

MRS PETERS   I don't know, unless it got sick and died. *(She reaches over and swings the broken door, then swings it again. Both women watch it.)*

---

[5]**Foster**   Minnie's name before she was married
[6]**reproach**   blame

MRS HALE	You weren't raised round here, were you? *(MRS PETERS shakes her head.)* You didn't know – her?
MRS PETERS	Not till they brought her yesterday.
MRS HALE	She – come to think of it, she was kind of like a bird herself – real sweet and pretty, but kind of timid and – fluttery. How – she – did – change. *(She pauses; then as if struck by a happy thought and relieved to get back to everyday things.)* Tell you what, Mrs Peters, why don't you take the quilt in with you? It might make up her mind.
MRS PETERS	Why, I think that's a real nice idea, Mrs Hale. There couldn't possibly be any objection to it, could there? Now, just what would I take? I wonder if her patches[7] are in here – and her things. *They look in the sewing basket.*
MRS HALE	Here's some red. I expect this has got sewing things in it. *(She brings out a fancy box.)* What a pretty box. Looks like something somebody would give you. Maybe her scissors are in here. *(She opens box.)* Why – *MRS PETERS bends nearer, then turns her face away.* There's something wrapped up in this piece of silk.
MRS PETERS	Why, this isn't her scissors.
MRS HALE	*(lifting the silk)* Oh, Mrs Peters – it's – *MRS PETERS bends closer.*
MRS PETERS	*(rising)* It's the bird.

---

[7]**patches**   pieces of material to be used in making the quilt

MRS HALE	*(jumping up)* But, Mrs Peters – look at it! Its neck! Look at its neck! It's all – other side to.[8]
MRS PETERS	Somebody wrung – its – neck.

Their eyes meet. A look of growing comprehension, of horror. Voices are heard outside. MRS HALE slips box under quilt pieces, and sinks into her chair. Enter SHERIFF and COUNTY ATTORNEY centre.

COUNTY ATTORNEY	*(as one turning from serious things to little pleasantries[9])* Well, ladies, have you decided whether she was going to quilt it or knot it? *(He crosses down left.)*
MRS PETERS	We think she was going to – knot it. *(She reseats herself.)*
COUNTY ATTORNEY	Well, that's interesting. I'm sure. *(Seeing the bird-cage.)* Has the bird flown? *(He moves above table to right centre.)*

---

[8]**other side to**   twisted back to front
[9]**pleasantries**   light-hearted conversation

MRS HALE   *(putting more quilt pieces over the box)* We think the – cat got it.

COUNTY ATTORNEY   *(preoccupied)* Is there a cat? *(He moves down right.)*

MRS HALE glances in a quick covert way at MRS PETERS.

MRS PETERS   Well, not now. They're superstitious, you know. They leave.

COUNTY ATTORNEY   *(to the SHERIFF, continuing an interrupted conversation)* No sign at all of anyone having come from outside. Their own rope. Now let's go up again and go over it piece by piece. *(They start upstairs.)* It would have to have been someone who knew just the –

The two women sit there not looking at one another, but as if peering into something and at the same time holding back. When they talk now it is in the manner of feeling their way over strange ground, as if afraid of what they are saying, but as if they cannot help saying it.

MRS HALE   She liked the bird. She was going to bury it in that pretty box.

MRS PETERS   *(in a whisper)* When I was a girl – my kitten – there was a boy took a hatchet, and before my eyes – and before I could get there – *(She covers her face an instant.)* If they hadn't held me back I would have – *(she catches herself, and looks where voices are heard off right, then falters weakly)* – hurt him.

MRS HALE   *(with a slow look round her)* I wonder how it would seem never to have had any children around. *(Pause.)* No, Wright wouldn't like the bird – *(she picks up the bird-cage)* – a thing that sang. She used to sing. He killed that, too.

MRS PETERS	*(moving uneasily)* We don't know who killed the bird.
MRS HALE	I knew John Wright.
MRS PETERS	It was an awful thing was done in this house that night, Mrs Hale. Killing a man while he slept, slipping a rope around his neck that choked the life out of him.
MRS HALE	His neck. Choked the life out of him.
MRS PETERS	*(with rising voice)* We don't know who killed him. We don't know.
MRS HALE	*(her own feeling not interrupted)* If there'd been years and years of nothing, then a bird to sing to you, it would be awful – still, after the bird was still.
MRS PETERS	*(something within her speaking)* I *know* what stillness is. When we homesteaded in Dakota, and my first baby died – after he was two years old, and me with no other then –
MRS HALE	*(moving)* How soon do you suppose they'll be through looking for the evidence?
MRS PETERS	I know what stillness is. *(Pulling herself together.)* The law has got to punish crime, Mrs Hale.
MRS HALE	*(not as if answering that)* I wish you'd seen Minnie Foster when she wore a white dress with blue ribbons and stood up there in the choir and sang. *(She rises and moves above the table, looking around the room.)* Oh, I *wish* I'd come over here once in a while! That was a crime! That was a crime! Who's going to punish that?
MRS PETERS	*(looking upstairs)* We mustn't – take on.

MRS HALE	I might have known she needed help! I know how things can be – for women. I tell you, it's queer, Mrs Peters. We live close together and we live far apart. We all go through the same things – it's all just a different kind of the same thing. *(Brushes her eyes, noticing the bottle of fruit,*[10] *reaches out for it.)* If I was you I wouldn't tell her her fruit was gone. Tell her it *ain't*. Tell her it's all right. Take this in to prove it to her. She – she may never know whether it was broke or not. *(She sits right of table.)*

MRS PETERS rises, takes the bottle, looks about for something to wrap it in; takes a petticoat from the clothes brought from the other room, and very nervously begins winding this about the bottle.

MRS PETERS	*(in a false voice)* My, it's a good thing the men couldn't hear us. Wouldn't they just laugh! Getting all stirred up over a little thing like a – dead canary. As if that could have anything to do with – with – wouldn't they *laugh*! *(She crosses to the fire and sits.)*

The men are heard coming downstairs.

MRS HALE	*(under her breath)* Maybe they would – maybe they wouldn't.
COUNTY ATTORNEY	*(crossing left above table)* No, Peters, it's all perfectly clear except a reason for doing it. But you know juries when it comes to women. If there was some definite thing. Something to show – something to make a story about –

---

[10]***the bottle of fruit***   Minnie's bottled fruit had frozen in the unheated house while she was in prison, as she feared it would

a thing that would connect up with this strange way of doing it –

The women's eyes meet for an instant. Enter HALE from outer door centre.

HALE *(up centre)* Well, I've got the team around. Pretty cold out there.

COUNTY ATTORNEY *(left)* I'm going to stay here a while by myself. *(To the SHERIFF.)* You can send Frank out for me, can't you? I want to go over everything. I'm not satisfied that we can't do better.

SHERIFF *(up right)* Do you want to see what Mrs Peters is going to take in?

The ATTORNEY goes to the table, picks up the apron, and laughs.

COUNTY ATTORNEY Oh, I guess they're not very dangerous things the ladies have picked out. *(He moves a few things about, disturbing the quilt pieces which cover the box. He then steps back.)* No, Mrs Peters doesn't need supervising. For that matter, a sheriff's wife is married to the law. Ever think of it that way, Mrs Peters?

MRS PETERS Not – just that way.

SHERIFF *(chuckling)* Married to the law. *(He moves towards the other room.)* I just want you to come in here a minute, George. We ought to take a look at these windows.

COUNTY ATTORNEY *(scoffingly)* Oh, windows! *(He crosses right above the table.)*

MRS PETERS rises and goes to above table centre.

SHERIFF	We'll be right out, Mr Hale.

HALE goes out centre. The SHERIFF follows the COUNTY ATTORNEY out right. Then MRS HALE rises, hands tight together, looking intensely at MRS PETERS, whose eyes make a slow turn, finally meeting MRS HALE's. A moment MRS HALE holds her, then her own eyes point the way to where the box is concealed. Suddenly MRS PETERS throws back the quilt pieces and tries to put the box in the bag she is carrying. It is too big. She opens the box and starts to take the bird out, but it goes to pieces and she stands there helpless. Suddenly there is a sound of voices in the other room. MRS HALE snatches the box and puts it in the pocket of her big coat. The COUNTY ATTORNEY and SHERIFF enter right.

COUNTY ATTORNEY	*(down right – facetiously)* Well, Henry, at least we found out that she was not going to quilt it. She was going to – what is it you call it, ladies?
MRS HALE	*(her hand against her pocket)* We call it – knot it, Mr Henderson.

Further reading

Trifles is an adaptation of *A Jury of Her Peers*, a short story based on an actual trial Susan Glaspell covered while working as a newspaper reporter. It can be found online. Other crime stories with a neat twist include Roald Dahl's short story *Lamb to the Slaughter* (1953), and many of the Sherlock Holmes stories by Sir Arthur Conan Doyle.

Saint Joan

by George Bernard Shaw

Saint Joan is set in the Middle Ages, during the wars between France and England. The French are ruled by a young prince Charles, the Dauphin, who is described by Shaw as 'a poor creature physically' with 'little narrow eyes, near together, a long pendulous nose that droops over his thick short upper lip, and the expression of a young dog accustomed to be kicked'. Joan, on the other hand, is a tough, vigorous teenager from the country, and she is determined to put some courage into the timid Dauphin.

At this point in the play, the court, having heard of Joan's arrival, decide to test whether she will recognise 'the blood royal'. The Dauphin hides and his place on the throne is taken by Bluebeard (Gilles de Rais).

On the right are two Chairs of State on a dais.[1] Bluebeard is standing theatrically on the dais, playing the king, and, like the courtiers, enjoying the joke rather obviously. There is a curtained arch in the wall behind the dais; but the main door, guarded by men-at-arms, is at the other side of the room; and a clear path across is kept and lined by the courtiers. Charles is in this path in the middle of the room. La Hire is on his right. The Archbishop, on his left, has taken his place by the dais: La Trémouille at the other side of it. The Duchess de la Trémouille, pretending to be the Queen, sits in the Consort's[2] chair, with a group of ladies in waiting close by, behind the Archbishop.

The chatter of the courtiers makes such a noise that nobody notices the appearance of the page at the door.

THE PAGE	The Duke of – *(Nobody listens.)* The Duke of – *(The chatter continues. Indignant at his failure to command a hearing, he snatches the halberd[3] of the nearest man-at-arms, and thumps the floor with it. The chatter ceases; and everybody looks at him in silence.)*

---

[1] **dais** platform
[2] **Consort** King's wife
[3] **halberd** long weapon, with an axe-head and spike at the top

Attention! *(He restores the halberd to the man-at-arms.)* The Duke of Vendôme presents Joan the Maid to his Majesty.

CHARLES   *(putting his finger on his lip)* Ssh! *(He hides behind the nearest courtier, peering out to see what happens.)*

BLUEBEARD   *(majestically)* Let her approach the throne.

Joan, dressed as a soldier, with her hair bobbed [4] and hanging thickly round her face, is led in by a bashful and speechless nobleman, from whom she detaches herself to stop and look around eagerly for the Dauphin.

THE DUCHESS   *(to the nearest lady in waiting)* My dear! Her hair!
All the ladies explode in uncontrollable laughter.

BLUEBEARD   *(trying not to laugh, and waving his hand in deprecation [5] of their merriment)* Ssh-ssh! Ladies! Ladies!!

JOAN   *(not at all embarrassed)* I wear it like this because I am a soldier. Where be Dauphin?
A titter runs through the Court as she walks to the dais.

BLUEBEARD   *(condescendingly [6])* You are in the presence of the Dauphin.

Joan looks at him sceptically [7] for a moment, scanning him hard up and down to make sure. Dead silence, all watching her. Fun dawns in her face.

JOAN   Coom, Bluebeard! Thou canst not fool me. Where be Dauphin?

---

[4] **bobbed**   cut short
[5] **deprecation**   disapproval
[6] **condescendingly**   treating her as beneath him
[7] **sceptically**   doubting what she sees

A roar of laughter breaks out as Gilles, with a gesture
of surrender, joins in the laugh, and jumps down from
the dais beside La Trémouille. Joan, also on the broad
grin, turns back, searching along the row of courtiers,
and presently makes a dive, and drags out Charles by
the arm.

JOAN   *(releasing him and bobbing him a little curtsey)* Gentle
little Dauphin, I am sent to you to drive the
English away from Orleans and from France,
and to crown you king in the cathedral at
Rheims, where all true kings of France are
crowned.

CHARLES   *(triumphant, to the Court)* You see, all of you: she
knew the blood royal. Who dare say now that
I am not my father's son? *(To Joan)* But if you
want me to be crowned at Rheims you must
talk to the Archbishop, not to me. There he is
(he is standing behind her)!

JOAN   *(turning quickly, overwhelmed with emotion)* Oh,
my lord! *(She falls on both knees before him, with*
bowed head, not daring to look up) My lord: I am
only a poor country girl; and you are filled
with the blessedness and glory of God
Himself; but you will touch me with your
hands, and give me your blessing, won't
you?

BLUEBEARD   *(whispering to La Trémouille)* The old fox blushes.

LA TRÉMOUILLE   Another miracle!

THE ARCHBISHOP   *(touched, putting his hand on her head)* Child: you are
in love with religion.

JOAN   *(startled: looking up at him)* Am I? I never thought of that. Is there any harm in it?

THE ARCHBISHOP   There is no harm in it, my child. But there is danger.

JOAN   *(rising, with a sunflush of reckless happiness irradiating her face[8])* There is always danger, except in heaven. Oh, my lord, you have given me such strength, such courage. It must be a most wonderful thing to be Archbishop.

The Court smiles broadly: even titters a little.

THE ARCHBISHOP   *(drawing himself up sensitively)* Gentlemen: your levity is rebuked by this maid's faith.[9] I am,

---

[8]***with a sunflush . . .***   she is so happy that her face lights up
[9]**your levity is rebuked . . .**   Joan's faith is a criticism of your lack of seriousness

God help me, all unworthy; but your mirth
is a deadly sin.

Their faces fall. Dead silence.

BLUEBEARD   My lord: we were laughing at her, not at you.

THE ARCHBISHOP   What? Not at my unworthiness but at her
faith! Gilles de Rais: this maid prophesied
that the blasphemer[10] should be drowned in
his sin –

JOAN   *(distressed)* No!

THE ARCHBISHOP   *(silencing her by a gesture)* I prophesy now that you
will be hanged in yours if you do not learn
when to laugh and when to pray.

BLUEBEARD   My lord: I stand rebuked.[11] I am sorry: I can say
no more. But if you prophesy that I shall be
hanged, I shall never be able to resist tempta-
tion, because I shall always be telling myself that
I may as well be hanged for a sheep as a lamb.[12]

The courtiers take heart at this. There is more tittering.

JOAN   *(scandalized)* You are an idle fellow, Bluebeard;
and you have great impudence to answer the
Archbishop.

LA HIRE   *(with a huge chuckle)* Well said, lass! Well said!

JOAN   *(impatiently to the Archbishop)* Oh, my lord, will
you send all these silly folks away so that I
may speak to the Dauphin alone?

---

[10]**blasphemer**   someone who insults religion
[11]**stand rebuked**   have been rightly told off
[12]**for a sheep . . .**   If I am going to die anyway, I might as well be hanged for
committing a great sin as for a small one

LA HIRE   *(goodhumoredly)* I can take a hint. *(He salutes; turns on his heel; and goes out.)*

THE ARCHBISHOP   Come, gentlemen. The Maid comes with God's blessing, and must be obeyed.

The courtiers withdraw, some through the arch, others at the opposite side. The Archbishop marches across to the door, followed by the Duchess and La Trémouille. As the Archbishop passes Joan, she falls on her knees, and kisses the hem of his robe fervently.[13] He shakes his head in instinctive remonstrance;[14] gathers the robe from her; and goes out. She is left kneeling directly in the Duchess's way.

THE DUCHESS   *(coldly)* Will you allow me to pass, please?

JOAN   *(hastily rising, and standing back)* Beg pardon, maam, I am sure.

The Duchess passes on. Joan stares after her; then whispers to the Dauphin.

JOAN   Be that Queen?

CHARLES   No. She thinks she is.

JOAN   *(again staring after the Duchess)* Oo-oo-ooh! *(Her awestruck amazement at the figure cut by the magnificently dressed lady is not wholly complimentary.)*

LA TRÉMOUILLE   *(very surly)* I'll trouble your Highness not to gibe at[15] my wife. *(He goes out. The others have already gone.)*

JOAN   *(to the Dauphin)* Who be old Gruff-and-Grum?

CHARLES   He is the Duke de la Trémouille.

JOAN   What be his job?

---

[13] *fervently*   very enthusiastically
[14] *remonstrance*   protest
[15] **gibe at**   mock, insult

CHARLES   He pretends to command the army. And whenever I find a friend I can care for, he kills him.

JOAN   Why dost let him?

CHARLES   *(petulantly*[16] *moving to the throne side of the room to escape from her magnetic field)* How can I prevent him? He bullies me. They all bully me.

JOAN   Art afraid?

CHARLES   Yes: I am afraid. It's no use preaching to me about it. It's all very well for these big men with their armor that is too heavy for me, and their swords that I can hardly lift, and their muscle and their shouting and their bad tempers. They like fighting: most of them are making fools of themselves all the time they are not fighting; but I am quiet and sensible; and I don't want to kill people: I only want to be left alone to enjoy myself in my own way. I never asked to be a king: it was pushed on me. So if you are going to say 'Son of St Louis: gird on the sword of your ancestors, and lead us to victory' you may spare your breath to cool your porridge; for I cannot do it. I am not built that way; and there is an end of it.

JOAN   *(trenchant*[17] *and masterful)* Blethers![18] We are all like that to begin with. I shall put courage into thee.

CHARLES   But I don't want to have courage put into me. I want to sleep in a comfortable bed, and not live

---

[16]*petulantly*   sulkily
[17]*trenchant*   direct and cutting
[18]**Blethers!**   Rubbish! (What a stupid thing to say!)

in continual terror of being killed or wounded. Put courage into the others, and let them have their bellyful of fighting; but let me alone.

JOAN   It's no use, Charlie: thou must face what God puts on thee. If thou fail to make thyself king, thoult be a beggar: what else art fit for? Come! Let me see thee sitting on the throne. I have looked forward to that.

CHARLES   What is the good of sitting on the throne when the other fellows give all the orders? However! *(he sits enthroned, a piteous figure)* here is the king for you! Look your fill at the poor devil.

JOAN   Thourt not king yet, lad: thourt but Dauphin. Be not led away by them around thee. Dressing up don't fill empty noddle.[19] I know the people: the real people that make thy bread for thee; and I tell thee they count no man king of France until the holy oil has been poured on his hair, and himself consecrated[20] and crowned in Rheims Cathedral. And thou needs new clothes, Charlie. Why does not Queen look after thee properly?

CHARLES   We're too poor. She wants all the money we can spare to put on her own back. Besides, I like to see her beautifully dressed; and I don't care what I wear myself: I should look ugly anyhow.

JOAN   There is some good in thee, Charlie; but it is not yet a king's good.

---

[19]**noddle**   head
[20]**consecrated**   here, it means: recognised by God as King

CHARLES   We shall see. I am not such a fool as I look. I have my eyes open; and I can tell you that one good treaty is worth ten good fights. These fighting fellows lose all on the treaties that they gain on the fights. If we can only have a treaty, the English are sure to have the worst of it, because they are better at fighting than at thinking.

JOAN   If the English win, it is they that will make the treaty: and then God help poor France! Thou must fight, Charlie, whether thou will or no. I will go first to hearten thee. We must take our courage in both hands: aye, and pray for it with both hands too.

CHARLES   (*descending from his throne and again crossing the room to escape from her dominating urgency*) Oh do stop talking about God and praying. I can't bear people who are always praying. Isn't it bad enough to have to do it at the proper times?

JOAN   (*pitying him*) Thou poor child, thou hast never prayed in thy life. I must teach thee from the beginning.

CHARLES   I am not a child: I am a grown man and a father; and I will not be taught any more.

JOAN   Aye, you have a little son. He that will be Louis the Eleventh when you die. Would you not fight for him?

CHARLES   No: a horrid boy. He hates me. He hates everybody, selfish little beast! I don't want to be bothered with children. I don't want to be a father; and I don't want to be a son: especially a son of St Louis.[21] I don't want to be any of these fine things you all have your heads full of: I want to be just what I am. Why can't you mind your own business, and let me mind mine?

JOAN   *(again contemptuous)* Minding your own business is like minding your own body: it's the shortest way to make yourself sick. What is my business? Helping mother at home. What is thine? Petting lapdogs and sucking sugar-sticks. I call that muck. I tell thee it is God's business we are here to do: not our own. I have a message to thee from God; and thou must listen to it, though thy heart break with the terror of it.

CHARLES   I don't want a message; but can you tell me any secrets? Can you do any cures? Can you turn lead into gold, or anything of that sort?

JOAN   I can turn thee into a king, in Rheims Cathedral; and that is a miracle that will take some doing, it seems.

CHARLES   If we go to Rheims, and have a coronation, Anne will want new dresses. We can't afford them. I am all right as I am.

JOAN   As you are! And what is that? Less than my father's poorest shepherd. Thourt not lawful owner of thy own land of France till thou be consecrated.

CHARLES   But I shall not be lawful owner of my own land anyhow. Will the consecration pay off

---

[21]**St Louis**   Louis IX, an earlier King of France and great leader

my mortgages?[22] I have pledged my last acre to
the Archbishop and that fat bully. I owe
money even to Bluebeard.

JOAN   *(earnestly)* Charlie: I come from the land, and
have gotten my strength working on the land;
and I tell thee that the land is thine to rule
righteously and keep God's peace in, and not to
pledge at the pawnshop[23] as a drunken woman
pledges her children's clothes. And I come from
God to tell thee to kneel in the cathedral and
solemnly give thy kingdom to Him for ever and
ever, and become the greatest king in the world
as His steward and His bailiff,[24] His soldier and
His servant. The very clay of France will become
holy: her soldiers will be the soldiers of God:
the rebel dukes will be rebels against God: the
English will fall on their knees and beg thee let
them return to their lawful homes in peace.
Wilt be a poor little Judas,[25] and betray me and
Him that sent me?

CHARLES   *(tempted at last)* Oh, if I only dare!

JOAN   I shall dare, dare, and dare again, in God's
name! Art for or against me?

CHARLES   *(excited)* I'll risk it, I warn you I shan't be able
to keep it up; but I'll risk it. You shall see.

---

[22]**mortgages**   he has borrowed money from people, agreeing that, if he cannot repay them, they will own his land
[23]**pledge at the pawnshop**   offer to a money-lender who can keep it if you
cannot repay the loan in time
[24]**steward . . . bailiff**   officials who look after and run someone else's business or land
[25]**Judas**   in the Bible, the disciple who betrayed Jesus

(Running to the main door and shouting) Hallo! Come back, everybody. *(To Joan, as he runs back to the arch opposite)* Mind you stand by and don't let me be bullied. *(Through the arch)* Come along, will you: the whole Court. *(He sits down in the royal chair as they all hurry in to their former places, chattering and wondering.)* Now I'm in for it; but no matter: here goes! *(To the page)* Call for silence, you little beast, will you?

THE PAGE   *(snatching a halberd as before and thumping with it repeatedly)* Silence for His Majesty the King. The King speaks. *(Peremptorily)*[26] Will you be silent there? *(Silence)*.

CHARLES   *(rising)* I have given the command of the army to The Maid. The Maid is to do as she likes with it. *(He descends from the dais.)*

           General amazement. La Hire, delighted, slaps his steel thigh-piece with his gauntlet.[27]

LA TRÉMOUILLE   *(turning threateningly towards Charles)* What is this? I command the army.

           Joan quickly puts her hand on Charles's shoulder as he instinctively recoils.[28] *Charles, with a grotesque effort culminating in an extravagant gesture,*[29] *snaps his fingers in the Chamberlain's face.*

---

[26]**Peremptorily**   expecting to be obeyed, allowing no argument
[27]**gauntlet**   heavy glove
[28]**recoils**   jumps back nervously
[29]**grotesque . . . gesture**   he looks ridiculous as he summons his courage to snap his fingers dramatically

JOAN   Thourt answered, old Gruff-and-Grum.
(*Suddenly flashing out her sword as she divines*[30] *that her moment has come*) Who is for God and His Maid? Who is for Orleans[31] with me?

LA HIRE   (*carried away, drawing also*) For God and His Maid! To Orleans!

ALL THE KNIGHTS   (*following his lead with enthusiasm*) To Orleans!

Joan, radiant, falls on her knees in thanksgiving to God. They all kneel, except the Archbishop, who gives his benediction[32] *with a sigh, and La Trémouille, who collapses, cursing.*

Further reading

To find out what happens to Joan, and how the people of the 20th century viewed her, read the rest of Shaw's play. If you would like to read another play by Shaw, try *Androcles and the Lion*. It is much shorter than *Saint Joan* and contains a lot of humour. There are many novels based on the story of Joan of Arc, one of the best known being by Mark Twain.

---

[30]*divines*   realises with a moment of inspiration
[31]**Orleans**   the French enjoyed their first major victory in the Hundred Years War when, inspired by Joan, they defeated the English at Orléans
[32]*benediction*   blessing

King Henry V

William Shakespeare

This extract covers several scenes from Act 4 of William Shakespeare's *King Henry V*. Henry has claimed that the French crown is rightfully his and has led an army to France.

In this first scene, Henry's tiny English army, exhausted, hungry and weakened by disease, faces the full might of the huge French force – fresh, well fed and confident of victory.

Scene 3

Enter GLOUCESTER, BEDFORD, EXETER, ERPINGHAM with all his host, SALISBURY and WESTMORLAND

GLOUCESTER	Where is the king?
BEDFORD	The king himself is rode to view their battle.[1]
WESTMORLAND	Of fighting men they have full threescore[2] thousand.
EXETER	There's five to one. Besides, they all are fresh.
SALISBURY	God's arm strike with us! 'Tis a fearful odds. God be wi'you, princes all. I'll to my charge. If we no more meet till we meet in heaven Then joyfully, my noble lord of Bedford, My dear lord Gloucester and my good lord Exeter, And my kind kinsman, warriors all, adieu.
BEDFORD	Farewell, good Salisbury; and good luck go with thee.

[1]**battle** army
[2]**threescore** sixty

EXETER   Farewell, kind lord. Fight valiantly today.

(Exit Salisbury)

And yet I do thee wrong to mind thee of it,
For thou art framed of the firm truth of valour.

BEDFORD   He is as full of valour as of kindness,
Princely in both.

Enter the KING

WESTMORLAND   O that we now had here
But one ten thousand of those men in England
That do no work today.

KING   What's he that wishes so?
My cousin Westmorland. No, my fair cousin.
If we are marked to die, we are enough
To do our country loss. And if to live,
The fewer men, the greater share of honour.
God's will, I pray thee wish not one man more.
By Jove, I am not covetous[3] for gold,
Nor care I who doth feed upon my cost.[4]
It yearns[5] me not if men my garments wear.
Such outward things dwell not in my desires.[6]
But if it be a sin to covet honour,
I am the most offending soul alive.
No, faith, my coz,[7] wish not a man from
      England.
God's peace, I would not lose so great an honour
As one man more, methinks, would share
      from me,

---

[3]**covetous** greedy
[4]**upon my cost** at my expense
[5]**yearns** bothers
[6]**... in my desires** Henry is not interested in material things like clothes
[7]**coz** cousin

For the best hope I have. Oh, do not wish one
    more!
Rather proclaim it, Westmorland, through my
    host
That he which hath no stomach[8] to this fight
Let him depart. His passport shall be made,
And crowns for convoy put into his purse.
We would not die in that man's company[9]
That fears his fellowship to die with us.
This day is called the Feast of Crispian.[10]
He that outlives this day and comes safe home
Will stand a-tiptoe when the day is named,
And rouse him at the name of Crispian.
He that shall see this day and live old age,
Will yearly on the vigil[11] feast his neighbours,
And say 'Tomorrow is Saint Crispian.'
Then will he strip his sleeve and show his scars,
And say 'These wounds I had on Crispin's day.'
Old men forget, yet all shall be forgot
But he'll remember, with advantages,[12]
What feats he did that day. Then shall our
    names,
Familiar in his mouth as household words,
Harry the king, Bedford and Exeter,
Warwick and Talbot, Salisbury and Gloucester,
Be in their flowing cups[13] freshly remembered.

---

[8]**stomach** 'guts'
[9]**We would not die . . .**   I do not want to die alongside any man who is
    afraid to die in my company
[10]**Crispian**   Crispin and Crispian were Roman shoemakers, put to death for
    their Christian faith; St Crispin's Day is 25 October
[11]**vigil**   night before the saint's day
[12]**advantages**   exaggerations
[13]**flowing cups**   toasts

This story shall the good man teach his son,
And Crispin Crispian shall ne'er go by
From this day to the ending of the world
But we in it shall be remembered.
We few, we happy few, we band of brothers –
For he today that sheds his blood with me
Shall be my brother; be he ne'er so vile
This day shall gentle his condition[14] –
And gentlemen in England, now abed,
Shall think themselves accursed they were not
        here,
And hold their manhoods cheap[15] whiles any
        speaks
That fought with us upon Saint Crispin's Day.

[14]**be he ne'er so vile . . .**   however low-born he might be, this day will turn
    him into a gentleman
[15]**hold their manhoods cheap**   consider themselves to be not real men

Enter SALISBURY

SALISBURY My sovereign lord, bestow yourself with speed.
The French are bravely in their battles set,
And will with all expedience[16] charge on us.

KING All things are ready, if our minds be so.

WESTMORLAND Perish the man whose mind is backward now!

KING Thou dost not wish more help from England,
coz?

WESTMORLAND God's will, my liege, would[17] you and I alone,
Without more help, could fight this royal battle!

KING Why, now thou hast unwished[18] five thousand
men,
Which likes me better than to wish us one.
You know your places. God be with you all.
Tucket. Enter MONTJOY.

MONTJOY Once more I come to know of thee, King Harry,
If for thy ransom thou wilt now compound[19]
Before thy most assurèd overthrow.
For certainly thou art so near the gulf
Thou needs must be englutted.[20] Besides, in
mercy,
The Constable desires thee thou wilt mind[21]
Thy followers of repentance, that their souls
May make a peaceful and a sweet retire[22]

---

[16]**expedience**   speed
[17]**would**   I wish
[18]**unwished**   wished away
[19]**ransom . . . compound**   agree how much will have to be paid for your
release after you are captured
[20]**englutted**   swallowed up
[21]**mind**   remind
[22]**retire**   retreat

From off these fields where, wretches, their
       poor bodies
Must lie and fester.

KING   Who hath sent thee now?

MONTJOY   The Constable of France.

KING   I pray thee, bear my former answer back.
Bid them achieve[23] me, and then sell my bones.
Good God, why should they mock poor
       fellows thus?
The man that once did sell the lion's skin[24]
While the beast lived, was killed with hunting
       him.
A many of our bodies shall no doubt
Find native[25] graves, upon the which, I trust,
Shall witness live in brass[26] of this day's work.
And those that leave their valiant bones in
       France,
Dying like men, though buried in your
       dunghills,
They shall be famed, for there the sun shall
       greet them
And draw their honours reeking up to heaven,
Leaving their earthly parts to choke your clime,[27]
The smell whereof shall breed a plague in France.
Mark then abounding[28] valour in our English,
That being dead, like to the bullet's crazing

---

[23]**achieve** overcome
[24]**did sell the lion's skin** One of Aesop's fables tells of a man who was nearly
   killed hunting a bear whose skin he had over-confidently already sold
[25]**native** in their own country
[26]**Shall witness live in brass ...**   their graves will have brass plates on
   them telling of their heroism
[27]**clime** climate, country
[28]**abounding** (1) abundant, plentiful; (2) which will rebound to harm you

Break out into a second course of mischief
Killing in relapse[29] of mortality.
Let me speak proudly. Tell the Constable
We are but warriors for the working day.[30]
Our gayness and our gilt are all besmirched[31]
With rainy marching in the painful field.
There's not a piece of feather[32] in our host
(Good argument, I hope, we will not fly)
And time hath worn us into slovenry.[33]
But by the mass, our hearts are in the trim,
And my poor soldiers tell me yet ere night
They'll be in fresher robes, or they will pluck
The gay new coats o'er the French soldiers'
    heads
And turn them out of service. If they do this –
As, if God please, they shall – my ransom then
Will soon be levied.[34] Herald, save thou thy
    labour.
Come thou no more for ransom, gentle herald.
They shall have none, I swear, but these my
    joints,
Which if they have, as I will leave 'em them,
Shall yield them little. Tell the Constable.

MONTJOY   I shall, King Harry. And so fare thee well:
Thou never shalt hear herald any more.

Exit

---

[29]**in relapse**   (1) while they are decaying; (2) by a deadly rebound
[30]**for the working day**   who 'mean business'
[31]**gayness . . . besmirched**   our decorations and gold are all made dirty
[32]**feather**   plume (for decorating their helmets)
[33]**slovenry**   sloppiness
[34]**levied**   Henry means that, after the English have robbed the defeated
    French, they will easily have enough to pay a huge ransom

KING   *(Aside)* I fear thou wilt once more come again
for a ransom.

Enter YORK

YORK   My lord, most humbly on my knee I beg
The leading of the vanguard.

KING   Take it, brave York. Now soldiers, march away,
And how Thou pleasest, God, dispose the day.

Exeunt

In Scene 4, which has been cut from this extract, one of Henry's soldiers, a coward called Pistol, manages to capture a Frenchman who
is an even bigger coward than he is!

Scene 5 shows a dramatic turnabout in the fortunes of the two
armies. Facing fierce resistance from the English, the French army is
soon in disarray.

Scene 5

Enter CONSTABLE, ORLÉANS, BOURBON, and RAMBURES

CONSTABLE   *O diable!*[35]

ORLÉANS   *O Seigneur! Le jour est perdu, tout est perdu!*[36]

BOURBON   *Mort de ma vie,*[37] all is confounded,[38] all!
Reproach and everlasting shame
Sits mocking in our plumes.

A short alarm

O méchante fortune![39] Do not run away.

CONSTABLE   Why, all our ranks are broke.

---

[35] *O diable!*   O, the devil!
[36] *O Seigneur . . .*   O lord! The day is lost! All is lost!
[37] *Mort de ma vie!*   Death of my life!
[38] **confounded**   lost
[39] *O méchante fortune!*   O, evil fate!

BOURBON	O perdurable[40] shame! let's stab ourselves. Be these the wretches that we played at dice for?
ORLÉANS	Is this the king we sent to for his ransom?
BOURBON	Shame, and eternal shame, nothing but shame! Let us die! In once more, back again, And he that will not follow Bourbon now, Let him go hence, and with his cap in hand Like a base pander[41] hold the chamber door, Whilst by a slave, no gentler[42] than my dog, His fairest daughter is contaminate.
CONSTABLE	Disorder, that hath spoiled[43] us, friend us now. Let us on heaps go offer up our lives.
ORLÉANS	We are enough yet living in the field To smother up the English in our throngs,[44] If any order might be thought upon.
BOURBON	The devil take order now! I'll to the throng. Let life be short, else shame will be too long.
	Exeunt

In Scene 6, Henry hears that the Duke of York has been killed. Suddenly there is the sound of a trumpet call.

Scene 6

Alarm

KING	But hark, what new alarum is this same? The French have reinforced their scattered men.

---

[40]**perdurable**   long-lasting
[41]**pander**   pimp (someone who controls prostitutes)
[42]**gentler**   nobler
[43]**spoiled**   ruined
[44]**throngs**   crowds

Then every soldier kill his prisoners.
Give the word through.

Exeunt

> The battle is as good as over. The French are defeated, but Llewellyn and Gower, two of Henry's captains, are furious that some of the retreating French have killed the boys guarding the English army's luggage train.

Scene 7

Enter LLEWELLYN and GOWER

LLEWELLYN   Kill the poys and the luggage! 'Tis expressly against the law of arms. 'Tis as arrant[45] a piece of knavery,[46] mark you now, as can be offert,[47] in your conscience now, is it not?

GOWER   'Tis certain. There's not a boy left alive, and the cowardly rascals that ran from the battle ha' done this slaughter. Besides, they have burned and carried away all that was in the king's tent, wherefore the king most worthily hath caused every soldier to cut his prisoner's throat. Oh, 'tis a gallant king!

Further reading

There are two Shakespeare plays which can be read as 'prequels' to *King Henry V*: the two parts of *King Henry IV*. In those plays Shakespeare depicts Henry's wild life as a teenager and his association with the fat knight Sir John Falstaff.

---

[45]**arrant**   notorious
[46]**knavery**   wickedness
[47]**offert**   offered (as an example)

Activities

Nicholas Nickleby

Before you read

1   During your school life you have had dozens of teachers. What makes an ideal teacher, in your opinion? Discuss your ideas.

What's it about?

2   Imagine that you were a school inspector who had visited Dotheboys Hall. Write a report in which you give reasons for closing it down. Include references to:
   - the kind of boy sent to the school
   - the boys' state of health
   - beatings and other ill-treatment
   - living conditions and food
   - the fees charged by Squeers
   - letters the boys send home
   - Squeers's teaching.

3   Re-read Scene 22. How do you think Squeers and his family would later describe what happened?

   Work in groups of six. Individuals take the parts of Squeers, Mrs Squeers, young Wackford, Fanny, Fanny's friend Tilda and Tilda's boyfriend John. Improvise a conversation in which the four members of the Squeers family are questioned by Tilda and John, and give their version of events.

Thinking about the text

4   In groups of seven or eight, make a list of the characters in Scene 10 as far as the blackout and then cast the scene. One person should play Squeers, another Nicholas. Others in the group will play two or three roles.
   a   First talk in pairs or threes about the characters you are playing. How will you get across Squeers's cruelty, for example, or the boys' misery?
   b   Then each 'cast' acts the scene to the rest of the class.
   c   Finally, talk as a class about the way David Edgar has turned Dickens's novel into a play. What are your favourite moments?

Treasure Island

Before you read

1 You might have read *Treasure Island*, the novel on which this play is based, or seen one of the *Pirates of the Caribbean* films. In small groups, talk about pirate stories that you know.
  ● What kind of people are pirates in these books and films?
  ● What do we expect of a pirate tale?

Make a list of the things that usually happen and the types of people who usually appear.

What's it about?

2 Long John Silver is one of the most famous characters in literature. What are our first impressions of him here?

In groups of six, read through the whole extract and decide what Silver is like. Find examples from the script which show him to be:
  ● friendly
  ● polite
  ● a good actor
  ● clever
  ● good with words
  ● kind and patient with Jim
  ● respected by other crew members as though he were the true captain.

Then perform the extract again, bringing out Silver's qualities.

Thinking about the text

3 The scene changes several times in the extract. It opens in the port at Bristol then moves to Trelawney's room on the harbour-side and then to Silver's inn, before the scene on-board ship.

Imagine you were going to perform this play at school. Design a simple stage set that would enable the action to move quickly from one location to another. Avoid complicated scene-changes; think particularly about the stage direction: *'ALL SAILORS create the impression of a ship.'*

Draw pictures or diagrams to show what the set would look like and write a paragraph explaining how the scene can change quickly from one location to another.

Trifles

Before you read

1   As a class, talk about crime and detective stories that you have read or seen on television.

   ● First think about stories in which a crime is uncovered when somebody finds evidence. For example, does anyone know any of the Sherlock Holmes stories, such as *The Speckled Band*?

   ● Then discuss stories in which the detective is mainly interested in the psychology of the criminals – their motives and the way they think.

What's it about?

2   Imagine you are defending Minnie Wright in court. Write the speech you will deliver to the jury when you sum up your case. Use whatever arguments you can to convince the jury that she is innocent, including the following:

   ● there was a gun in the house
   ● Minnie had no known motive
   ● there were no signs of a fight or anger
   ● Minnie was 'timid'.

3   In small groups discuss why the play is called *Trifles*. Think about the following questions:

   ● Why do the men laugh when they come downstairs to overhear Mrs Hale ask 'I wonder if she was goin' to quilt it or just knot it?' (page 107)?

   ● What different attitudes do the men and women have towards the fact that Mrs Peters has decided to take Minnie an apron and some bottled fruit (pages 116 and 117)?

   ● What is the effect of the play's final line (think about the possible double meaning)?

   ● What motive might Minnie have had for killing her husband?

Thinking about the text

4   The stage directions are extremely important in this play, especially those describing the behaviour and motives of Mrs Peters and Mrs Hale. In pairs, look at pages 108–109. Talk about the importance of the following stage directions and what they reveal about the characters:

- *they look at each other, then start to glance back at the door.*
- *mildly*
- *nervously*
- *Suddenly stopping and leaning forward.*
- *MRS HALE starts to say something, looks at MRS PETERS, then goes on sewing.*

Act out the block of stage directions at the end of the play (page 118). You will need a cardboard box and a few pieces of cloth as props. Follow the stage directions very carefully. As you act, try to think what is in your character's mind.

5   Both women know that it is wrong to tamper with potential evidence at the scene of a murder, but they still hide the canary.

   a   In small groups, discuss how the following moments in the play prepare us for what the two women are going to do:
   - Mrs Hale pulls out the bad stitching and then re-sews it herself
   - Mrs Hale hides the box when the men come back and lies about the cat getting the bird
   - Mrs Peters tells a story from childhood about a boy killing her kitten
   - Mrs Hale comments that Wright 'killed' Minnie's singing
   - Mrs Peters recalls what it was like after her first baby died
   - Mrs Hale wishes that Mrs Peters had seen Minnie in the choir.

   b   Discuss what you think is in the women's minds when they decide to hide the dead canary.

Saint Joan

Before you read

1   In this extract the Dauphin makes a momentous decision when he agrees to be crowned and lead his country.

Think of a moment you have read about in history or mythology when someone made a similarly crucial decision which proved to be a turning-point. Talk to a partner about the decision and what then happened.

What's it about?

2   How do you think Joan realises that Bluebeard is not the Dauphin, and then picks out the real Dauphin? Discuss in pairs whether she has special powers, or is simply using common sense.

3   a   List four or five of Joan's statements which show that she hasn't any embarrassment or nervousness among courtiers and isn't impressed by their rank.
    b   Which character is she impressed by? How can we tell?

4   Joan, the Dauphin, Bluebeard and the Archbishop are all different and distinctive characters. In groups of five, read from the beginning to the top of page 124 (one person reads the Duchess, La Trémouille and La Hire). Talk about the different ways in which each of the four main characters speaks and behaves. Then act out the section in order to bring out the differences.

5   What do the following people think of Joan by the end of the scene:
   ● the Dauphin
   ● the Duchess
   ● the Archbishop?

Thinking about the text

6   At the beginning of the scene, the Dauphin does not want to be King. Why not? How does Joan persuade him?

7   Look at the way Joan speaks. How has Shaw managed to get across the idea that Joan is a simple country girl?

King Henry V

Before you read

1   In a group, talk about war films that you have seen and list the characters in them who might be called 'leaders'. For each character, make a note of:
   ● their most important actions as leaders
   ● the human qualities they displayed (such as courage, in its many forms).

   Of all of them, who would you select as the most successful leader, and why?

What's it about?

2   Read the beginning of Scene 3 up to Henry's entrance, page 133. What is the mood among the English generals? How can you tell?

3   Henry's words to his men (Scene 3, pages 133–135) are sometimes called 'the Saint Crispin's Day speech'. What does he say to lift his soldiers' spirits? For example:
   ● In what ways does he play upon the men's sense of honour?
   ● Where does he embarrass any men who might have thought about deserting the army?
   ● What does he say about future ages and fame?
   ● How does he use the disadvantage of their small numbers to establish unity?

Thinking about the text

4   The French leaders are contrasted with the English. In what ways do they fail as leaders?

5   Shakespeare rarely paints a clear black-and-white picture of his characters. In what ways does Henry seem to you to be less than perfect as a leader? For example, in Scenes 6 and 7, two different reasons are given to explain why Henry ordered his men to kill their prisoners.

   What do you think was the real reason? And was he right to do so? Talk about this as a class. Was Henry 'a gallant king' or a war criminal who killed unarmed prisoners?

Compare and contrast

1   In each of these plays a character faces a turning point in his or her life where they must make a difficult decision.

Working in small groups, devise a radio interview with two or more of the characters. Write a script in which the interviewer asks each person:
- What challenge did you face?
- How did you deal with it?
- What did you feel afterwards? Do you think you did the right thing?

Record the interviews or perform them for the class.

2   These extracts feature some famous fictional characters such as Nicholas Nickleby, Squeers and Long John Silver; and equally famous figures from history – Saint Joan and King Henry V.

Select two: the one you most admire and the one you least admire. Write a short essay explaining your choices.

3   All of these extracts include moments of dramatic tension, when the audience is wondering what will happen next and how things will turn out.

In pairs, compare two of the extracts and talk about the ways in which the authors create tension and keep the audience interested.

4   Choose two extracts that you particularly enjoyed reading and write a short essay comparing them. Use these questions to help you:
- What are the two extracts about?
- What are the main characters like?
- How are the texts similar and how are they different?
- What do you notice about the language used in each text?

3 Deception

A huge number of plays through the ages have been about deception of one kind or another. We see women disguising themselves as men; crooks pretending to be honest; cowards boasting about their bravery. In fact, one of the main lessons that plays can teach us is that appearances are often very different from reality.

The extracts in this section show that deceiving people need not always be wrong. They also show that stories about deceivers can be extremely funny.

Activities

1   In pairs, talk about a time when you deceived somebody.
    - What was the situation?
    - Why did you think that deceiving them was a good idea?
    - What happened – were you found out or did the deception succeed?
    - Did you feel at all guilty about it afterwards?

2   In groups, make a list of characters who have successfully deceived others. Your examples can come from books, plays, films or television. Each person should then pick their favourite deceiver and explain their choice to the others. What do your chosen deceivers have in common? How are they different?

3   Write a short scene involving two people in which one tries to deceive the other. For example, your two characters could be a child and a parent, an employee and a boss or something more unusual such as a disguised alien trying to pass as human. Decide at the beginning whether your scene is to be serious or comic. Remember to set it out in play form.

Lad Carl

by John O'Connor

| This complete play is based upon an old Scandinavian folk tale about a boy who sets off one day to become a thief-catcher.

Scene 1

Early morning in winter. A courtyard of a peasant's cottage in a small village somewhere in Scandinavia, many centuries ago. Grettir is pumping water. Her son Carl enters from the house, stuffing clothes into a canvas bag, and carrying a wooden slatted box, inside which we hear a pigeon cooing.

GRETTIR   *(looking up, but carrying on with her pumping)*

What do you mean, you're going to be a thief-catcher?

CARL   A thief-catcher. Catch thieves.

GRETTIR   But it's not a career.

CARL   I don't see why not. Harald's a dog-catcher. Sveinn catches fish. I'll be a thief-catcher.

GRETTIR   You'll come to no good.

CARL   I'll come to no good stuck here, mother. Look, I'll give it a try for a year. If it doesn't work out, I'll come home and get a job on the farm.

GRETTIR   But why do you have to go now? It's winter. There's no one on the roads. You'll freeze before you get to town. At least stay till the spring.

CARL   No. My mind's made up. If I don't go now, I'll be stuck here for ever. *(Picking up the box.)* Come on, pigeon.

GRETTIR   Do' know why you want that daft pigeon. First chance he gets he flies back to the village.

CARL   Oh, company. I'll write to you, I promise.

He walks off and turns to take a farewell look at the cottage.

GRETTIR   Fat chance.

CARL   Wish me luck.

GRETTIR   Luck. *(As he leaves she calls after him.)* You'll need it. *(She picks up her full pail and goes off towards the house, stops and then calls out after him as the lights dim.)* And don't take the mountain road – it's infested with wolves!

The lights dim to the terrifying sound of wolves howling.

Scene 2

As the wolf howls die away, the lights come up on the interior of a mountain cabin. Apart from a table and some chairs, there are stuffed animals' heads on the walls, together with a collection of axes, pikes and guns and an old clock. A fire burns in the grate but it is partially obscured by a clothes-horse covered in washing.

Outside the wind blows more powerfully than before. There is a knocking at the door. Then another. After a few seconds Carl enters, covered in snow. He looks around cautiously and, closing the door after him, strides over to the fire to warm himself.

CARL   *(calling out)*

Hello. Anyone at home?

Receiving no reply, Carl takes his coat off and throws it over a chair. He sits down and is about to remove his boots when a voice says:

VOICE   I wouldn't stay here if I were you.

He looks around, but sees no-one.

CARL   Sorry?

Thurid, an old woman, appears from behind the clothes-horse, where she has been sitting on a stool.

THURID   I said I wouldn't stay here if I were you. This is a thieves' lair, this is.

CARL   Ah, good evening, mother. I was wondering if I might have a bed for the night. It's bitter out there.

THURID   A thieves' lair.

CARL   Really? You wouldn't have anything hot to eat, I suppose? I can pay . . . though I haven't much.

He pulls a small leather bag from inside his shirt, opens it and a single coin falls out onto the table. Carl regards it apologetically; the old woman treats it with the disdain[1] that it deserves.

---

[1]***disdain***   the old woman doesn't think much of it!

THURID   Thieves. Violent, merciless and unscrupulous.

CARL   *(as though they are three names he can't quite place)*
            Don't think I've heard of them. Come to
            think of it, forget the food – I've a crust in my
            bag will keep me going. What I really need is a
            good sleep. Bedrooms up here, are they?

            *And he picks up his luggage – the bag and the pigeon in its
            box – and ascends the stairs, while Thurid, muttering
            away to herself, collects the washing from the clothes-horse
            and folds it up.*

THURID   . . . Unscrupulous, reckless and devil-may-care.

            *As she works, we hear the sound of approaching horses,
            closely followed by men's voices, arguing. The door
            bursts open and the thieves enter, clearly in a bad
            mood.*

GRIM   I told you it would be a waste of time. Who
            would be travelling on a day like this?

THORGAUT   My information was –

GRIM   Your information! It was your information
            that had us waiting three days for –

THORGAUT   They were held up. I cannot be held respons-
            ible for –

GRIM   You're supposed to be our leader, aren't you?
            Who else do we hold responsible? You're our
            (sarcastically) 'captain'.

THORGAUT   Do you want the job?

GRIM   Well I couldn't make a worse –

            He breaks off: Skapti has found Carl's coat.

SKAPTI   *(to Thurid)* What's this?

THURID   Traveller. *(She nods over her shoulder and they all look up in the direction of the rooms upstairs, forgetting their arguments for a moment.)*

JOKULL   Any money?

She picks up the single coin from the table and shows it to them.

THURID   Oh, and a pet pigeon.

SKAPTI   Does he know about us?

THURID   *(Nods.)* I told him: cunning, depraved and ruthless. *(Muttering as she leaves:)* Wouldn't listen, though.

JOKULL   What do we do?

GRIM   Throw him down the ravine.

SKAPTI   Feed him to the wolves.

JOKULL   Drown him.

GRIM   *(to Thorgaut)* You're 'captain' – you decide.

But, before another argument can get under way, Carl's voice is heard from the top of the stairs.

CARL   Good evening. We haven't met, but my name is Carl. *(Calmly he descends and joins them.)* I think I must have another name, but I'm damned if I know what it is. Mother always calls me 'Lad Carl'. I was wondering – you wouldn't have a vacancy for a trainee thief, I suppose?

Blackout.

Scene 3

Later that night. When the lights go up we see that Carl is tied to a chair and gagged. The thieves are sitting around and look as though they have been discussing something for a long time.

JOKULL   Or drop boulders onto him from a great height.

SKAPTI   Eaten by bears. That's always plausible.

THORGAUT   But what if he isn't a spy? What if –

GRIM   Of course he's a spy. We are the notorious Shadowdale Gang – (*He rips a Wanted poster off the wall and reads:*) 'terrorisers of the border settlements'. Five times the farmers have sent out vigilantes[2] to catch us and each time we have evaded them. We are cunning.

THURID   Ruthless and devil-may-care.

GRIM   In their frustration the authorities have come to realise that their only chance to catch us is to infiltrate our operation.[3]

THORGAUT   He doesn't look like a spy.

GRIM   What do you expect? A black hat and a cloak?

THORGAUT   I mean he's skinny and underfed. He looks more like . . . well, a thief.

SKAPTI   Why don't we set him a test? A kind of trial. We give him a job to do. If he does it, he's in. If he fails, we kill him. Easy.

THORGAUT   What sort of trial?

---

[2]**vigilantes**   unofficial police
[3]**infiltrate our operation**   get someone who will join our gang and then spy on us

SKAPTI   I have received information –

GRIM   Oh, not you as well!

THORGAUT   Shut up, Grim, and listen.

SKAPTI   I have received information that old Hallbjorn plans to take one of his oxen to market tomorrow. If Lad Carl here wants to prove he's genuine about becoming a thief, all he has to do is steal it.

There is a silence as they all mull this over.

GRIM   I'm uneasy.

JOKULL   So what's the alternative?

THORGAUT   All right. See what he says.

They remove Carl's gag.

Did you hear all that?

CARL   Certainly. When do I start?

Blackout.

Scene 4

It is dawn the next morning and the light comes up on a track through the mountain pass. The weather has improved and there is the sound of bird song. Carl enters from the right, jumps up onto a boulder and looks off behind him. After a second or two he hears the sound that he is waiting for: an ox bellowing. He jumps down from the rock, reaches into his bag and produces a colourfully decorated leather shoe, which he places carefully in the middle of the path. Checking once more that his man is on his way, Carl hides behind the boulder and waits.

Hallbjorn the farmer enters from right, pulling on a rope, which suddenly tightens, forcing him to an unexpected standstill. Not in the best of tempers – it is a long haul from his valley farm, over the mountains to market – he jerks angrily on the rope. The ox bellows offstage but nothing happens. Hallbjorn is about to go back and discipline the animal when he notices the shoe.

HALLBJORN   Hello! What a very handsome shoe.

He picks it up and examines it admiringly.

Now if there were a pair, I'd take them home to my wife. As it is . . .

He throws the shoe away and trudges off left, pulling on the rope.

Come on, Daisy!

Daisy is clearly some way behind, because she is still not in sight by the time Hallbjorn has disappeared offstage left. While all we can see is the rope stretched across the stage, tightening and slackening as the tired Hallbjorn pulls his reluctant animal to market, Carl leaps out from behind the boulder, retrieves the shoe and exits after the farmer. The lights fade just as Daisy is about to enter on the end of the rope . . .

Scene 5

A minute later: the same path, a hundred paces further on. Carl enters, right. Checks over his shoulder as before, deposits the shoe again and hides behind another convenient boulder. The farmer enters as before, pulling on the rope, and immediately spots the 'second' shoe.

HALLBJORN   Well, I'll be . . . If it isn't the other half of the pair. *(He looks back over shoulder wistfully.)* This is too good to miss. *(Idea!)* I know what. I'll tie my ox to this boulder and nip back for the other shoe. My wife will be delighted!

Hallbjorn loops the rope around Carl's boulder and exits right. Carl nips out, loosens the rope and exits after the farmer. Offstage there is the sound of bellowing, followed by the clatter of heavy oxen hooves receding into the distance.

Hallbjorn re-enters, holding only one shoe and scratching his head. It takes him only a second to realise what has happened.

Oh, no! She'll kill me! *(He beats his head with his fist.)* Think, think, think! *(A second idea!)* Yes! I'll nip back to the farm, collect our other ox and take that to market instead. Daisy might be lost, but at least I can get a good price for Bluebell. Then, when I get back tomorrow, I'll blame her for letting Bluebell get stolen from under her nose while she slept . . .

Mulling over the finer points of his plan in his head, Hallbjorn turns back and sets off on his secret mission to collect the second ox as the lights fade . . .

Scene 6

The lights go up on the cabin interior and a burst of celebratory song from the gang — something like 'For he's a jolly good fellow!'.

CARL   Thank you, gentlemen. And, if I know Hallbjorn, I'm pretty confident that I can predict what he will do tomorrow . . .

They fill their cups and toast him again as the lights fade.

Scene 7

Dawn the following day. Lights up on the mountain path, as before, and Hallbjorn enters, pulling on his rope — as before. He stops to mop his brow and sits on a tree-stump.

HALLBJORN   Just about here I found that confounded shoe and lost Daisy. *(Looking over his shoulder.)* I'll be damned if they catch me with that trick again. *(Producing a heavy hunting rifle from his pack, he shouts out, challengingly, to anyone within earshot.)* Just come and try, that's all!

Suddenly, from somewhere behind him, there is the sound of a hoarse bellowing. He sits up and listens, hardly able to believe his ears. There is a second bellow.

My lost ox! *(Leaping to his feet.)* Coming, Daisy, my love! Daddy's on his way!

He hurriedly ties the rope round the tree-stump and runs off left, in the direction of the sound. Carl enters cautiously from right, unties the rope, picks up the discarded gun and exits. A second later we hear another bellow (more realistic this time) and the sound of heavy ox-hooves galloping off into the distance.

Hallbjorn re-enters, exhausted, perspiring and depressed.

It must have been the wind. Never mind. Come on Bluebell . . . Bluebell? Oh no! I don't believe this. Bluebell! Bluebell!

And, as the lights dim, the poor farmer runs off in vain pursuit of his second lost ox.

Scene 8

The cabin interior, later that night. The thieves have plainly been celebrating again and are now relaxing, relishing their new recruit's success and dreamily contemplating a very rosy future indeed. Carl sits at the head of the table, basking in their adulation.[4]

SKAPTI   Two oxen in two days!

JOKULL   It's a miracle.

CARL   Not at all, gentlemen. Simply a combination of good intelligence and animal cunning.

THURID   *(In admiration)* Ruthlessness and devil-may-care bravado.

GRIM   Welcome to the Shadowdale Gang, Lad.

SKAPTI   So what's our next job?

An embarrassed silence falls. They all realise that Thorgaut has been standing aloof.

---

[4]*adulation*   overdone praise and flattery

THORGAUT   Don't look at me. You have a new leader now: 'Lad' Carl. Ask him.

They look back at Carl. The lights dim as he begins his reign as the thieves' new leader.

CARL   Well, gentlemen, the way I see it is this . . .

Music. The lights go to blackout . . .

Scene 9

When the lights come up on the cabin, it is a scene of quiet industry — much poring over maps and stacking of ropes, weapons and baskets full of provisions.

CARL   *(Calling them together)* So. One final recap just to check everything's clear. Grim?

GRIM   We assemble on the ridge above the village. Our signal to attack is the hooting of an owl and the cry of a wolf following the final chime of the church clock at midnight.

CARL   Skapti?

SKAPTI   The parish tax collections are in the strong-room in the assembly house. The only guard will be Agnar, an old caretaker, probably asleep.

CARL   Jokull?

JOKULL   We break in through the small window at the back, and overpower the old man.

CARL   And Thorgaut?

Thorgaut does not reply immediately. Either he is still resentful at having lost the leadership of the gang, or something is troubling him.

Thorgaut?

THORGAUT You and I break the lock of the front door
          from the inside –

GRIM And we drag the coffers out onto the sledge –
      and away.

CARL Excellent. Any questions?

THORGAUT Just one. You haven't said what we do with
          Agnar, the old caretaker.

SKAPTI Kill him. Something quiet.

JOKULL Tie him up and dump him out the back – let
        him freeze to death.

GRIM Whatever happens, we can't afford to leave
      him there to identify us.

      They all look at Thorgaut.

CARL Thorgaut?

THORGAUT *(He has made an important decision.)* No. He's an old
          man. It's not right.

GRIM That doesn't usually bother you.

THORGAUT It bothers me today: I say no violence.

          They are interrupted as the clock begins to chime.

CARL Eleven o'clock. Load the sledge, then let's be
      about it.

      *They collect their equipment and all leave the cabin except
      for Carl, who goes upstairs. In the silence of the now empty
      room we hear, from somewhere above, the flapping of a
      bird's wings. As Carl comes back down the stairs,
      Thorgaut returns for his gun and the two men find them-
      selves facing each other. Carl smiles, slaps Thorgaut on the
      shoulder and exits. Thorgaut, still troubled, collects his gun
      and follows, as the lights dim to blackout.*

Scene 10

In almost complete blackness we can just make out that we are in a large tim-bered hall. A village clock chimes twelve. We hear the hooting of an owl and the howling of a wolf; then, a few seconds later, the sound of wood being splintered. A rectangular patch of starry sky appears in the back wall and a shadowy figure climbs through the window. He helps in three others and they stand, waiting for orders. When they speak, it is in tense whispers.

GRIM'S VOICE   Which way's the strong-room, Carl?

SKAPTI'S VOICE   He said straight in front.

JOKULL'S VOICE   As far as I can make out, that's just a blank wall.

THORGAUT'S VOICE   This doesn't feel right . . . Carl? . . . Lad?

There is a deafening and blinding burst of gunfire, then silence.

Carl enters, carrying a torch, which illuminates the scene. Grim, Skapti and Jokull lie dead in a pool of blood; Thorgaut is slumped against the back wall, not wounded, but totally stunned and incapable of movement. Appearing from behind the heavy assembly house furniture are six villagers, carrying still smoking guns.

Hallbjorn enters and hands Carl a slatted box. Carl lifts it to his face and we can just hear a gentle cooing and the fluttering of wings.

Thorgaut staggers forward and stares long and hard into Carl's face.

THORGAUT   You betrayed us . . . We trusted you.

Carl says nothing, but takes some seed from his pocket and feeds the pigeon. As the lights dim to blackness, we hear the peaceful sound of the bird as it settles down for the night inside its wooden cage.

Further reading

Lad Carl is based on a traditional tale from Scandinavia. If you want to read more, look at *Scandinavian Folk and Fairy Tales* by Mary McBride and Claire Booss (Crown Publishers, 1988). This play comes from an anthology of three short plays, all linked by the same theme and called *Crimes and Punishments* (Nelson Thornes, 2000).

The Wind in the Willows

adapted by Alan Bennett
from the novel by Kenneth Grahame

This is an extract from an adaptation of the popular children's book *The Wind in the Willows* staged by the National Theatre in 1990.

Despite the best efforts of his friends Rat, Mole and Badger, Toad has been sent to prison for stealing a car.

Part Two

These days on offender of Toad's social position and financial resources[1] could expect to be sent directly to an open prison, but Toad's prison is anything but open. He has the dungeon to himself, it's true, but Toad is not at the moment disposed to look on the positive side. Dressed in the traditional prison garb[2] of overalls printed with broad (green) arrows he sits on his little bench contemplating his lot with no equanimity[3] at all. Were there a psychiatrist attached to this gaol he would diagnose Toad[4] as 'subject to violent mood swings'.

TOAD   Poor Toad. Poor little Toady. All aloney. On his owney. Nobody wants him. Nobody cares. I had a big house once. Servants. Friends. Wise old Badger. Clever intelligent Rat. Sensible little Mole. Why did I not listen to you? O foolish, foolish Toad. It's the end of everything. At least it's the end of Toad, which comes to the same thing. Thrust into this dark, damp dungeon, despised by the world, deserted by his friends, whom he entertained entirely at his own expense. Ungrateful Badger.

---

[1] *financial resources*   money and savings
[2] *garb*   clothing, uniform
[3] *equanimity*   composure, calmness when under stress
[4] *diagnose Toad*   describe what was wrong with Toad

Sanctimonious[5] Rat. Silly Mole. Where are they when I need them? All nice and snug at home while I'm stuck here for twenty years. Twenty years! Oh, it's not fair. *(He goes into a paroxysm[6] of grief, kicking his legs and banging his fists on the ground.)* I can't bear it.

There is a shaft of light as the Gaoler's Daughter comes in with a plate.

G'S DAUGHTER   Dinner.

TOAD   Dinner? *Dinner!* At a time like this? I couldn't. *(Pause.)* What is it?

G'S DAUGHTER   Bubble and squeak.[7]

TOAD   Bubble. And squeak. How insensitive people are. No. No. Never.

G'S DAUGHTER   I'll take it away then.

TOAD   *(hastily) No.* I might just manage to force down a mouthful. After all, I owe it to my friends. *(Snuffling, he takes a mouthful or two.)*

G'S DAUGHTER   You like that?

TOAD   Not particularly.

G'S DAUGHTER   Oh well. *(She makes to take it away again.)*

TOAD   No. I mean I don't dislike it. It's perfectly acceptable, in its way. Only, it's not what I'm used to at Toad Hall.

G'S DAUGHTER   Toad Hall? Tell me about Toad Hall.

---

[5]**Sanctimonious**   smug, superior, self-righteous, 'holier-than-thou'
[6]**paroxysm**   fit
[7]**Bubble and squeak**   fried-up mashed potatoes and cabbage

TOAD	Toad Hall is a self-contained gentleman's residence in a picturesque riverside setting. It is very unique in its way and though parts of it date back to the fourteenth century it has up-to-the-minute sanitation and the last word in billiard rooms.[8]
G'S DAUGHTER	It sounds paradise.
TOAD	Toad Hall? *(airily)* No. Just a well-run gentleman's residence.
G'S DAUGHTER	I wish I could see it, Toady. *(When all's said and done he is rather a pet.)*
TOAD	I wish I could take you there, my dear. *(She's a comely enough lass.)*
	They cuddle.
	Who knows? Perhaps one day I can find you a position below stairs.[9]
	They uncuddle smartish.
G'S DAUGHTER	Below stairs? You're a convict. You're in here for twenty years.
TOAD	I was forgetting. Twenty years? Twenty years!
G'S DAUGHTER	There, there. I'm a fool to myself, I know, but I've got a real soft spot for you.
TOAD	I know. So many people do. It's known as charm.
	He blows his nose vigorously and while he doesn't quite examine the results, it's still a bit off-putting.

---

[8]**Toad Hall is a self-contained ...**   Toad's description sounds like an estate agent's advertisement
[9]**below stairs**   as a servant

G'S DAUGHTER	I just wish I could think of a way of getting you out of here.
	There is a distant call, echoing down the prison corridors: WASHING! BRING OUT YOUR WASHING!
	Here comes my aunt. She's a washerwoman.
TOAD	Think no more about it. I have several aunts who ought to be washerwomen.
	The call gets closer. WASHING! PUT OUT YOUR WASHING.
G'S DAUGHTER	She washes for all the convicts in the castle.
TOAD	How lovely for her . . . all those terrible vests and big men's smalls.
	The Washerwoman comes into the dungeon.
G'S DAUGHTER	*(thoughtfully)* Actually, you're not unlike one another . . .
TOAD	I beg your pardon?
G'S DAUGHTER	*(still thoughtful)* Only she can come and go as she pleases . . .
TOAD	Lucky her.
	You can see what's coming and I know it's no business of mine but prisoners in plays and operas so often escape by getting round gaolers' daughters that you'd think that for gaolers daughterlessness would have long ago become part of the job specification.
G'S DAUGHTER	*(decisively)* Listen Toad. You're very rich and aunty's very poor.
TOAD	That's the way the world is, I'm afraid. Aunty is doubtless carefree and happy, whereas we rich are burdened with our

responsibilities. I myself am on the
board of several companies.

G'S DAUGHTER   What I mean, silly, is that if you made it worth
her while, she might lend you her clothes and
you could escape disguised as her. Aunty!

TOAD   Me dress up as a washerwoman? What a dis-
tasteful idea.

*But the Gaoler's Daughter is already explaining her plan
to Aunty.*

Couldn't I be a lady novelist . . . or a high
born prison visitor? I mean *her*?

WASHERWOMAN   Him? I don't see the likeness at all.

G'S DAUGHTER   *(mouthing)* Give her some money.

*Toad, never quick on the uptake where self-preservation is
concerned, doesn't immediately twig.[10] The Gaoler's
Daughter mimes bribery.*

TOAD   Oh yes, sorry *(giving her a coin)*.

WASHERWOMAN   I do begin to see a distant resemblance.

More money changes hands.

Yes. Come to think of it we could be sisters.

G'S DAUGHTER   Now, aunty – the first thing is to change your
clothes.

WASHERWOMAN   What for? It's not Friday.

TOAD   The disguise, madam.

G'S DAUGHTER   Undress.

WASHERWOMAN   Here? I'm a married woman.

---

[10]**twig**   understand

| TOAD | Are you stupid or something? You've had your money. |

WASHERWOMAN Oh yes. That's it, isn't it! You've been paid. Now take your clothes off! Very well, but only to my bloomers. A line's got to be drawn somewhere. *(She begins to undress – an awesome[11] sight.)*

TOAD Believe me, madam, this is far more distressing for me than it is for you. They're so smelly.

WASHERWOMAN I wash other people's clothes. I'm not paid to wash my own.

G'S DAUGHTER Now we'll tie you up.

WASHERWOMAN Tied up? You didn't say anything about being tied up.

TOAD Let me. They'll imagine I overpowered her.

WASHERWOMAN Get off me.
She sends Toad flying.

G'S DAUGHTER Aunty, you've been paid, behave.

WASHERWOMAN I don't care. The nasty little blighter, I'll . . .

TOAD That's enough out of you, madam.
Toad puts a laundry bag over the Washerwoman's head, which puts paid to further argument.

G'S DAUGHTER Now Toad. Put the dress on. You'll make a very good woman.

TOAD Yes. I'm not unattractive . . . though I'm not sure this is really my colour.

---

[11]**awesome**   very impressive, breathtaking

G'S DAUGHTER   You look just the ticket.[12] Aunty, stop moaning.
                A furious grunt.

                I don't think it will be difficult to get past the
                guard. My aunt is a woman of unblemished[13]
                reputation and a keen Methodist and the
                guard is sure to keep his distance.

TOAD   What do you mean, keep his distance?

G'S DAUGHTER   Well, you know men. So good luck, little toad,
                and if you get back to your nice house
                remember the humble gaoler's daughter who
                took a fancy to you.

TOAD   I shall. I shall. Perhaps when I open the house
                to ordinary people, you can come over to tea.
                Bye bye to Aunty.
                The sack lunges blindly at Toad but happily misses.

---

[12]**just the ticket**   perfect
[13]**unblemished**   unstained

This is a far, far better thing you do than you ever did before. Free at last! And now I must make a beeline for home where I can get out of this malodorous[14] frock. And how convenient! A railway station.

A train has arrived, stopped and the Train Driver jumped down to polish his engine.

TRAIN DRIVER   Hello, mother, you don't look very happy.

TOAD   Oh, sir, I am a poor washerwoman who's lost all her money and can't get home.

TRAIN DRIVER   Dear me. And you've got kiddies waiting for you, I dare say.

TOAD   Nine of them. At least. There may be more, only they never keep still long enough for me to count them. And they'll be hungry and playing with matches and getting their little heads stuck fast in the railings. Oh dear, oh dear.

TRAIN DRIVER   Tell me, do you wash a good shirt?

TOAD   Shirts are my speciality. Shirts are to me, sir, what daffodils is to Wordsworth.[15]

TRAIN DRIVER   Well, I'll tell you what I'll do. I go through a power of shirts in this job. So if you'll wash me a few when you get home, I'll give you a ride on the engine.

TOAD   Oh, sir, thank you, sir.

TRAIN DRIVER   Hop on.

---

[14]**malodorous**   smelly
[15]**daffodils . . . Wordsworth**   the poet Wordsworth wrote a famous poem called 'Daffodils'

TOAD   Well, I won't hop on. If I *hopped* on somebody
                    might think I was a frog or something of that
                    kind. The idea! Ha ha! There we are.

TRAIN DRIVER   Comfy? Off we go.

                    *There's a rush of steam, the sound of wheels, a whistle and
                    the train is off.*

TOAD   Oh, isn't this exciting . . . the fields, the trees,
                    the world flying past. This is the way to
                    travel! Tell me, Mr Engine Driver, how much
                    would an engine like this cost?

TRAIN DRIVER   Cost? You're not thinking of buying one?

TOAD   Me, a poor washerwoman, how could I?

TRAIN DRIVER   You'd have to wash a deal of shirts before you
                    saved up for one of these. I say, that's
                    unusual, the signal's against us.

                    *We see a signal fall and the train screeches to a halt. The
                    Train Driver gets down and presses his ear to the ground.
                    He peers back the way they have come.*

                    Funny. We're the last train running in this
                    direction tonight and yet I could swear we're
                    being followed.

TOAD   Followed?

TRAIN DRIVER   Yes. By another train. I'm sure of it.

TOAD   Well, let's get on then.

TRAIN DRIVER   No, no. I can't go against the signal. I can see
                    it now, there is another train. It's full of people.
                    Ancient warders,[16] policemen and shabbily

---

[16]**warders**   prison guards

dressed men in bowler hats, obvious and unmistakable plain clothes men even at this distance, and all of them shouting 'Stop, Stop'.

DISTANT CRIES	Stop, stop!
TOAD	Go, go! Oh, please go.
TRAIN DRIVER	Washerwoman, have you been telling me the truth?
TOAD	Yes. No. Oh, save me, dear kind Mr Engine Driver. I am not the kindly simple attractive laundress that I seem to be. I am a toad . . . the well-known and popular Mr Toad, of Toad Hall in the County of Berkshire. I have only this afternoon escaped from a noisome[17] dungeon into which, should that train catch up with us, I shall shortly be thrust again. Let me fling myself on your mercy, kind engine driver . . .
TRAIN DRIVER	Here, steady on, steady on. What were you in prison for?
TOAD	Borrowing a motor car.
TRAIN DRIVER	I don't hold with motor cars.
TOAD	Nor do I.
TRAIN DRIVER	There's too many of them for my money.
TOAD	I do so agree.
TRAIN DRIVER	Railways not roads is my motto.
TOAD	My sentiments exactly.

---

[17]**noisome**   disgusting

TRAIN DRIVER	Doubtless those people following us are all outraged motorists.
TOAD	Yes. Sports car drivers, horn sounders . . .
TRAIN DRIVER	Representatives of the AA and the RAC and others of their vile breed. Well, Toad, I ain't going to be the one to hand you over to the four-wheeled fraternity.[18] So listen carefully. I'm going to start the engine, turn my back and when I turn round again you will, to my utter surprise, have jumped off the train and disappeared. You understand me?
TOAD	Oh yes.

The Train Driver turns his back, only Toad, who hasn't understood him, is still there.

TRAIN DRIVER	I said 'I'm going to turn my back and when I turn round again you will, to my utter surprise . . .'
TOAD	Oh, sorry. *(He jumps down as the signal changes.)*
TRAIN DRIVER	Toodloo, Toad. Now I'm going to lead them a right dance.

The Train Driver reverses his engine and goes back to meet the oncoming train. There is a sound of two massive engines grinding to a halt and then a moment later motorists, ticket collector, policeman and warders rush on pursued by the crazed car-hating Train Driver wielding an axe. When he has chased them all from the stage Toad slowly raises his head and finds himself looking up into the enquiring face of Albert.

ALBERT	Hello, Toad.
TOAD	I beg your pardon.

---

[18]**four-wheeled fraternity**   people who love cars (i.e. those chasing Toad)

ALBERT   I said 'Hello, Toad'.

TOAD   Toad? I'm a washerwoman.

ALBERT   Yes, and I'm Sherlock Holmes. It's not another one of your crazes, is it? Caravans, cars and now dressing up in women's clothing.

TOAD   Ssh. This is my disguise.

ALBERT   Well, I've penetrated[19] it.

TOAD   Who are you?

ALBERT   You don't recognise me? I'm not in disguise. I'm one of your ex-employees. Albert.

TOAD   Albert, of course. My trusty steed. My long-lost friend.

ALBERT   Cue for bottom-smacking.

Toad smacks his bottom.

TOAD   What are you doing here?

ALBERT   After the caravan incident my doctor advised me to seek employment in a less, as it were, stressful occupation, and preferably one where motor cars didn't come up behind me and without so much as a by your leave[20] biff me on the bottom. Hence the barge now coming slowly round the bend. The lady on the barge is the barge lady, my new employer. Virginia Woolf[21] she isn't, but her pie and peas is to cooking what

---

[19]**penetrated**   seen through
[20]**a by your leave**   asking permission
[21]**Virginia Woolf**   a famously clever novelist

Michelangelo[22] was to ceiling painting.
I will introduce you.

TOAD   No, no. She mustn't know we know each
other. There, there, old fellow. *(He starts smacking
Albert's bottom.)*

ALBERT   *(under his breath)* Don't *do* that.

BARGEWOMAN   Nice morning, ma'am.

TOAD   Is it? Not for a poor washerwoman who this
very morning got a letter from her married
daughter telling her to drop everything and
come at once. Are you a mother, ma'am?

BARGEWOMAN   I was once. Where was this married daughter
of yours living, ma'am?

TOAD   Near the river, ma'am, not far from an
elegant, self-contained gentleman's residence
called Toad Hall. Perhaps you've heard of it?

BARGEWOMAN   Toad Hall? I certainly have. And it just so happens I'm headed that way myself. Hop on the
barge. One more don't make no difference to
Albert.

ALBERT   Oh no. And why draw the line at one? One
washerwoman doesn't make no difference . . .
why not offer a lift to the entire staff of the
Snow White Laundry? Plus their dependent[23]
relatives. Albert doesn't mind. The more the
merrier.

---

[22]**Michelangelo**   a famous artist who painted the ceiling of the Sistine
Chapel in Rome
[23]**dependent**   whom they look after and support

BARGEWOMAN	He's cheered up. He was very depressed earlier on. So, you're in the washing line, ma'am?
TOAD	Yes. One is a career woman, for one's sins.
BARGEWOMAN	Are you *very* fond of washing?
TOAD	I love it. Love it. It's my vocation.[24] Laundry is my life!
BARGEWOMAN	Well, what a blessing it is that I met you. We can both do each other a good turn.
TOAD	*(nervously)* In what way, precisely?
BARGEWOMAN	Why, my washing, silly, a whole heap of my scanties[25] and whatnot.
TOAD	Scanties?
	She gets him his tub, washboard and a packet of Rinso soapflakes.
BARGEWOMAN	There you are . . . the tools of your trade. The raw materials of your art.
TOAD	Well, I suppose any fool can wash.
BARGEWOMAN	I bet you can't wait. Look at these . . . it's a laundress's banquet.
TOAD	I don't feel very well. *(Toad starts to rinse and scrub with no great enthusiasm and a great deal of slopping the water about and general mess, while at the same time getting tied up in the stuff that he's washing and gradually getting furiouser and furiouser.)*

---

[24]**vocation**   career, job someone is destined to do
[25]**scanties**   underwear

BARGEWOMAN   *(singing)*

> Happy to float
> In a lazy old boat
> On a lovely sunny day.
> Drifting along,
> Singing a song
> Wash all your troubles away
> Completely. Happy to glide
> As you go with the tide,
> As you wend[26] your weary way,
> Drifting along
> As you're singing a song
> On this lovely sunny day

This traditional ballad comes to an abrupt end when Toad hangs the washboard on the line rather than the washing, a departure from established laundry procedures[27] that convinces the Bargewoman of something she has suspected for some time.

Ha ha ha. I've been watching you. You're never a washerwoman. I bet you've never washed so much as a dishcloth all your life.

TOAD   Don't take that tone with me, madam. Washerwoman? No, I am not a washerwoman. I am Toad, the well-known and distinguished Toad, the landed proprietor.[28] I'm under a bit of a cloud at present but I'm still streets ahead of you . . . a common bargewoman.

BARGEWOMAN   A toad? Why so you are. Ugh. A horrid crawling toad and in my nice clean barge too. Now

---

[26]**wend**   go, travel
[27]**departure from established laundry procedures**   Toad's methods are different from the way laundry is normally done!
[28]**landed proprietor**   land-owner and businessman

that's something I will not have. *(She grabs hold of Toad and thrusts him overboard.)* Over you go! and good riddance! Ugh, what a nasty, scaly hand.

TOAD   Did you see that? Did you see it?

ALBERT   Why, laundry person, I see you're wet through! (Notice how I'm keeping up your disguise.)

TOAD   There's no need to, stupid. She's twigged that I'm a toad.

ALBERT   I'm not surprised. You never deceived me for a minute.

Toad starts undoing Albert's harness.

Here, what're you doing?

TOAD   I'm riding you back to Toad Hall.

ALBERT   You can't do that.

BARGEWOMAN   Stop that. Stop that this minute.

ALBERT   I've got a bad back. Besides, I'm quite happy here. My only complaint is that it lacks a bit of civilisation.

BARGEWOMAN   Albert. It's a toad. That washerwoman is a toad.

Now that Albert is out of harness the barge naturally begins to drift, so the Bargewoman has to leap for the bank and grab the tow rope herself. Meanwhile Toad tries unsuccessfully to mount the horse.

TOAD   I'll give you civilisation. I'll give you as much civilisation as you want.

ALBERT   Can I have the run of the library?

TOAD Yes, yes.

ALBERT And you won't object if I put my nose in a book?

TOAD No.

ALBERT Because I like a bit of Tennyson[29] now and again.

TOAD She's got out of the barge.

BARGEWOMAN Listen, you horrible toad. That horse is my property.

ALBERT Property? I'm not your property. I'm not anybody's property. You'd better get on, Toady. Her property indeed. All property is theft.

They gallop off and the Bargewoman, unable to follow because she is still tethered to her tow rope, promptly bursts into tears. Two young rabbits come innocently along trailed by the Chief Weasel and Weasel Norman. Suddenly the two weasels bring out bags of sweets which they offer to the rabbits, who, very sensibly, scream in terror and take to their heels. Only then does the Chief Weasel notice the blubbering Bargewoman.

CHIEF WEASEL The good lady seems a trifle upset. Perhaps you should enquire why. And, Norman, sensitively.

WEASEL NORMAN Hello, darling. Why the waterworks?

BARGEWOMAN I haven't got anybody to pull my barge.

WEASEL NORMAN Come again, my love?

[29]**Tennyson** a Victorian poet

BARGEWOMAN   I've been robbed.

WEASEL   The stupid cow's been robbed, Chief.
NORMAN

CHIEF WEASEL   Who by, Norman?

WEASEL   Who by, my little slice of suet pudding?
NORMAN

BARGEWOMAN   A toad – he stole my horse.

WEASEL   A likely story. A toad stealing a horse . . . a
NORMAN   toad! A toad, Chief. You don't think . . . ?

CHIEF WEASEL   Just ask her which way it went, Norman.

BARGEWOMAN   That way.

                They rush off after Toad.

                *Having eluded their pursuers Toad and Albert come upon
                a Gypsy eating stew from a pan.*

TOAD   Can you smell something?

ALBERT   Well it's not me.

TOAD   Stew. I smell stew.

                Toad and Albert walking along.

                Good evening, Mr Gypsy.

GYPSY   Good evening, washerwoman.

TOAD   That looks a lovely stew. I could do with some
                stew.

GYPSY   Want to sell that there horse of yours?

TOAD   What? Me sell this beautiful young horse of
                mine? Oh no. It's out of the question.

ALBERT   I should think so too.

TOAD   Shut up. I'm far too fond of him, and he simply dotes on me. *(He smacks Albert on the bottom.)*

GYPSY   I'll give you a shilling a leg.

TOAD   A shilling a leg. Ah.

ALBERT   What're you up to?

TOAD   Shut up, I'm counting. *(He counts the legs.)* It appears to come to two, but I think it should come to four, but I could never think of accepting only four shillings for a horse like this.

ALBERT   I should think not.

TOAD   Keep quiet.

GYPSY   Five . . . and that's 3/6 more than it's worth.

ALBERT   It's a scandal.

TOAD   Ssh. I have a plan. Look here, gypsy. This is my final offer: 6/6[30] cash down plus as much stew as I can possibly eat in that pot. It's a Prize Hackney.[31]

GYPSY   It's a wicked price. All right.

Toad is given his stew while the Gypsy examines Albert's teeth, smacks his bottom, etc. Toad pats Albert.

---

[30]**3/6 . . . 6/6**   three shillings and sixpence . . . six shillings and sixpence (equivalent to about seventeen pence and thirty-two pence in today's money)

[31]**Hackney**   special kind of horse used for drawing carriages

TOAD   Goodbye, old friend.

ALBERT   *Goodbye?* I thought you said you had a plan.

TOAD   Yes, that was it. 6/6 and as much stew as I could possibly eat.

ALBERT   But what about me?

TOAD   Albert. You will have to stop thinking about yourself all the time. It creates a very unfortunate impression. Goodbye.

ALBERT   Toad!

TOAD   Don't work too hard.

ALBERT   Why did I let Toad take me in? I was happy pulling the barge. I was happy in my meadow at Toad Hall. Now I shall have to plod round back streets and pull a rag and bone cart[32] for the rest of my days, never more to gallop in green fields.

GYPSY   Come on you.

The Gypsy hauls Albert away.

Further reading

The play from which this extract is taken is based on Kenneth Grahame's 1908 novel, *The Wind in the Willows*. There is another play, *Toad of Toad Hall*, by A. A. Milne. This is also based on the novel but concentrates on the escapades of the infamous Mr Toad.

---

[32]**rag and bone cart**   cart for collecting things that people have thrown out but which can be re-sold

Blackadder: Potato

by Richard Curtis and Ben Elton

This extract is from *Potato*, an episode in the second series of the BBC television comedy *Blackadder*. Sir Walter Raleigh has triumphantly returned from his voyages to the New World. The Queen is thrilled, not least because Raleigh has made her a gift of a new and fascinating vegetable: the potato. Sick of Raleigh's popularity with the Queen, Blackadder boasts that he is himself about to undertake a life-threatening round-the-world voyage – and is then forced to go through with it after the Queen promises to marry him when he returns. His friend Lord Percy is terrified at the prospect, despite encouragement from Blackadder's sidekick Baldrick.

(Cut to Percy and Baldrick in a room. Baldrick is folding what appear to be sheets. Perhaps they are sails)

PERCY   *(petulantly¹)*. I'm not coming. I'm just not coming. I mean, of course I'm very *keen* to go on the trip, it's just . . . unfortunately, uh . . . I've got an appointment . . . to have my nostrils plucked . . . next year.

BALDRICK   Oh, I'm sorry, my lord. I thought it was because you were a complete coward.

PERCY   *(sounding nervous)* Don't be ridiculous, Baldrick . . . You know me, I mean . . . I laugh in the face of fear, and tweak the nose of the dreadful spindly killer fish. I'm not one of your milksops² who's scared out of his mind by the mere sight of water. Gah! *(backs away in fear as Baldrick holds out a goblet of water to his face)* Yes,

---

¹**petulantly**   like a spoilt child
²**milksop**   cowardly weakling

all right, I admit it, I admit it, I'm terrified! You see, Baldrick, when I was a baby, I was savaged by a turbot.[3] Oh, Baldrick, you can't think of a plan to get me out of this, can you?

BALDRICK   Uh, you can hide, my lord.

PERCY   Hide. Brilliant! Where? *(They look around the room. The trunk the sheet came from is standing invitingly wide open)*

BALDRICK   Um . . . *(After a few minutes, Baldrick finally sees the box)* In the box!

PERCY   Which one?! *(Figures it out).* Ah – perfect! *(Gets in the box)* Let's practise. All right, Edmund comes in and says, "Hello, Baldrick. You haven't seen Percy, have you?" And you say . . .

BALDRICK   Uh. *(Thinks hard)* No, my lord, I haven't seen him all day.

PERCY   Brilliant! *(They hear a door slam)* Oh my God, here he comes! *(Baldrick helps close the box lid on top of him)*

(Enter Blackadder. Baldrick is standing conspicuously[4] in the middle of the room next to the box)

BLACKADDER   Oh, hello, Balders. Where the hell's that cretin[5] Percy; you haven't seen him, have you?

(Baldrick can't remember what he was supposed to say. He thinks about it. Finally, with an air of blustery[6] triumph, he says)

BALDRICK   Yes, my lord! He's hiding in the box!

---

[3] **turbot**   a type of fish
[4] **conspicuously**   very noticeably
[5] **cretin**   idiot
[6] **blustery**   proud and boastful

BLACKADDER   *(eyeing the box)* Come on, jellybrain. Hurry up, otherwise we'll miss the tide! *(kicks the box, in the manner of, "is there anybody home?!")*

Blackadder's plan is to hire a ship, sail round the back of the Isle of Wight, and hide for a while. Unfortunately he enlists the services of the eccentric and clueless Captain Rum, and they end up going a lot farther than he had planned. Two years pass and the Queen, now bored with Raleigh, is beginning to miss Blackadder, despite the attentions of her chief minister, Lord Melchett, and her loyal Nursie, now engaged to marry Captain Rum.

(Caption appears,

"Two Years Later"

Then we see a very disgruntled[7] Raleigh wearing a dunce's outfit,[8] with the Queen throwing rings at his cap, and Melchett and Nursie looking on)

QUEEN   Where are they now?

MELCHETT   Well, Madam, if they haven't been eaten by cannibals, they should be back any minute now.

(The door bursts open and Blackadder, Percy and Baldrick make their entrance, bowing to the Queen)

EDMUND   Ma'am!

QUEEN   *(shrieks)* Edmund! You're alive!

EDMUND   *(patronizingly,[9] as if to shrug it off)* Oh, yes.

QUEEN   And your silly friend.

---

[7]**disgruntled**   fed up
[8]**dunce's outfit**   this includes a pointed hat with a large D on it, worn as a punishment to indicate stupidity
[9]**patronizingly**   in a very superior way

PERCY   Lord Percy, Ma'am *(bowing again)*.

QUEEN   And your monkey!

BALDRICK   *(bowing)* Your Majesty.

QUEEN   But where is Captain Rum?

BLACKADDER   Uh, bad news, my Lady; Rum is dead. *(Nursie screws her face up and starts to cry)*

PERCY   Do not despair, good woman. He died a hero's death: giving his life that his friends might live.

BLACKADDER   And that his enemies might have something to go with their potatoes.

NURSIE   You mean they put him in the pot?

BLACKADDER   Yes, your fiancé was only a third-rate sailor, but a first-rate second course. *(Nursie starts sobbing again)* However, we did manage to save something of him as a memento.[10] *(reaches in a large sack they brought in with them, takes out Rum's beard, and presents it to Nursie)* There.

NURSIE   Oh, my lucky stars; I shall wear it always, to remind me of him *(she puts it on)*.

BLACKADDER   However, Ma'am, I am now returned, and my mind cannot help remembering talk of wedding bells.

QUEEN   No, I am completely bored with explorers! And if you haven't brought me any presents, I'm going to have you executed!

BLACKADDER   Ma'am?

---

[10]**memento**   reminder, souvenir

QUEEN   I only let Raleigh off because he blubbed[11] on his way to the block. Presents, please!

BLACKADDER   Ah yes, Ma'am. *(he backs away, clearly trying to think of a plan)* Um, yes. Well, there was one thing, Ma'am, a most extraordinary gift from the island paradise we visited.

QUEEN   Hurry up!!

BLACKADDER   *(reaches into a sack Percy is holding and draws out a boomerang and hands it to her)*.

QUEEN   What is it?

MELCHETT   A stick.

QUEEN   *(threateningly)* Is it a stick, Lord Blackadder?

---

[11]**blubbed**   cried

BLACKADDER	Ah yes, Ma'am, but it is a very special stick. Because when you throw it away, it comes back!
QUEEN	Well, that's no good, is it; because when *I* throw things away, I don't *want* them to come back!! *(turns to Percy)* YOU!! Get rid of it!
PERCY	Certainly, Ma'am *(meekly takes it from her and tosses it behind him)*
QUEEN	What else have you brought?
BLACKADDER	Um, yes, well, there was very little time what with picking the weevils[12] out of biscuits and–
QUEEN	–Melchy, what did I do with that spare death warrant?
	(The boomerang comes back and hits Percy on the head, knocking him down. The Queen changes her mind on the stick)
QUEEN	Oh, Edmund, it's wonderful!

Further reading

There were four Blackadder series, each set in a different historical period. While each included actual historical and literary figures, they were always presented in a humorous and lighthearted fashion. The fourth series, set in the trenches of the First World War, has a powerful and poignant final scene.

---

[12]**weevils**   beetles that infested ship's food

The Foreigner

by Larry Shue

Charlie is depressed. To cheer him up and give him a break, his friend Froggy takes him to the United States for a few days to stay in a boarding house out in the country run by an old friend, an elderly widow called Betty.

But Charlie refuses to cheer up, because he regards himself as boring and hates meeting people. To save Charlie from having to make conversation with Betty and her other guests, Froggy makes out that Charlie is a foreigner who speaks no English. Charlie quickly fits into his role as 'the foreigner' and soon finds that everybody in the boarding house tells him their secrets, believing that he can't understand a word they're saying.

The house-guests include a young woman called Catherine and her younger brother Ellard. Everybody, including Catherine, has always believed Ellard to be a bit 'slow'. But the day after Charlie's arrival, Catherine comes downstairs to find that Ellard has been teaching 'the foreigner' English.

CATHERINE   Ellard?

ELLARD   Huh?

CATHERINE   What're you doin'?

ELLARD   We're workin' on some words. He wanted to.

CATHERINE   Oh . . .

ELLARD   Show you, look. Ready to do some words, Charlie? *(Points.)* What's that?

CHARLIE   'So-fa'?

ELLARD   'Sofa,' yep. An' what's that?

The '-ARD' in Ellard's name is pronounced as it is in 'Leonard', but so that you can hear the 'R' before the final 'D'. Charlie and Froggy are Londoners; everybody else is American and speaks with a southern drawl.

CHARLIE   'Rug'?

ELLARD   Uh-huh.

CATHERINE   Well, Ellard?

ELLARD   *(Pointing.)* What's that?

CHARLIE   'Stovva'?

ELLARD   'Stove'?

CHARLIE   'Stove'?

ELLARD   Yeah? That's good.

CATHERINE   Well, Ellard, I declare.

ELLARD   What's this here?

CHARLIE   Ahh . . .

ELLARD   *(Giving a hint.)* Ends with 'Ump.'

CHARLIE   'Lay-ump'?

ELLARD   'Layump,' that's right.

CATHERINE   Ellard, you taught him to say all these words?

ELLARD   Yeah.

BETTY   *(Coming into the room.)* Woo-oo! I found it, Charlie! I'd gone 'n' put it away with Meeks's stuff. *(Seeing the others.)* What in the world – ?

CATHERINE   Ellard's teachin' Charlie.

BETTY   He *is*?

ELLARD   'Kay, Charlie, here's some new ones. *(Holding up a rock.)* 'Rock'?

CHARLIE   'Rock'?

ELLARD	'Bush'?
CHARLIE	'Boosh'?
BETTY	Well, my land.
ELLARD	'Brick'?
CHARLIE	'Breek'?
CATHERINE	*(To Betty.)* What's that?
BETTY	Oh, Charlie seemed t' want t' hear some harmonica music, so I said –
CATHERINE	You play that?
BETTY	Well – useta could. I think I better go off 'n' practice somewheres, though.
CATHERINE	*(Starting into the kitchen, suppressing a smile.)* My my. A day for surprises.

When Froggy returns to check on Charlie, he is surprised to find that his 'shy and boring' friend is getting on very well indeed . . .

BETTY	This here's Charlie's friend, that brung him up here.
FROGGY	'At's right, Charlie? *(To Betty.)* 'Ow's it goin', then?
BETTY	Jest grand. Yes, sir. Couldn't be better. Ever'thing's fine.
FROGGY	Really?
BETTY	Yes, indeedy!
FROGGY	But I thought – .
BETTY	Oh, I know. But with Charlie around, ye jest sorta ferget about the bad things, don't ye?

FROGGY   Yer do?

BETTY   Oh, yes. Oh, Frog – you 'uz jest plain wrong, about Charlie. *(To the others.)* He said Charlie was jest gonna be real quiet-like, 'n' reg'lar, 'n' borin'. *(Charlie looks at Froggy, genuinely offended.)*

ELLARD   What!

CATHERINE   No!

BETTY   That's what he said! You believe it? *(To Froggy.)* Well, not to us he ain't. No, sir. Why, I don't reckon a minute goes by, but one of us catches Charlie doin' somethin' er sayin' somethin' real cute an' strange. Wearin' his little head-glass[1] at breakfast?

'Wearin' his little head-glass   Ellard and Charlie had been playing a 'mirror-game' in which one person imitates everything the other does; Betty had come in at a moment when Charlie and Ellard had placed their glasses on their heads and thought it was one of Charlie's foreign customs

FROGGY   Wearin' is little wot?

BETTY   No, Charlie ain't borin' at all. No, sir. Charlie, he's – why, he's jest simply – .

CHARLIE   Remarkable. *(Froggy reacts.)*

BETTY   Remarkable. Yes.

FROGGY   Well! *(Smiling, surprised.)* I thought e'd be a bit shy around 'ere. In 'is native country, of course, I know 'e's quite the, eh – the raconteur.[2]

BETTY   The what?

FROGGY   You know – jokes. Amusin' stories. *(Going to the bar for a drink.)* Oh, yes, quite the entertainer back 'ome, they tell me. But 'ere, I thought – .

BETTY   *(To Charlie.)* Oh, tell one!

CHARLIE   *(Falsetto.)* Hm?

BETTY   *(Almost jumping up and down.)* Tell one of yer – . *(To Froggy.)* Make him tell one of his stories!

FROGGY   Oh no, I didn't mean – .

BETTY   Oh, please! Go on, ask him!

CHARLIE   Oh – .

FROGGY   Well – .

BETTY   *(To Ellard and Catherine.)* Y'all listenin'? Charlie's gonna tell one o' his favorite stories! This is the chance of a lifetime! *(To Froggy.)* Go on!

---

[2]**raconteur**   skilled story-teller

FROGGY   Oh, well – uh, Charlie – ?

CHARLIE   Hm?

FROGGY   Is this all right? I mean, eh – poko dum fun-
nostoros? *(There being no way out, Charlie acquiesces[3]
graciously, though nervously.)*

CHARLIE   Ah – blasny, blasny. Eh – .

FROGGY   *(Going for drinks.)* Sorry, mate.

CHARLIE   Eh –. *(Experimentally.)* Brope snyep, snyope ss – .
(Starts over.) Breez *neez*-nyeep, sneep – . *(No
good. Clears throat. Froggy hands him a whiskey. He
downs it in one gulp, concentrates, and starts – slowly
at first.)*

Mirduschki omni   ('In the little town of
   bolyeeshnya,   Merridew
mirlo aramznyi   (there lived a little
   bro-o-oach   o-o-old
   peevno . . .   woman . . .
(In a quavering falsetto.)
'Zhmeetna! Zhmeetna!
Zhmeetna! Zhmeetna!'
(Narrator voice again.)
Do – du berznoznia   *(And* – her beautiful
   dottsky, Marla. . . .   daughter, Marla. . . .
(With appropriate gestures.)
Ah! Byootsky dottsky!   (Ah! A beautiful
   Perch damasa   daughter! But as
   baxa raxa. Hai.   stupid as a stone . . .
(In a silly, youthful falsetto.)

---

[3]**acquiesces**   reluctantly agrees

'Mirlo *meech*no, mirlo em?' dichni Marla omsk, 'y preeznia praznia, preeznia praznia, preep?'

("I'm heading out now, Mom," said Marla, "and trade these cheeses for some fine buttons."'
... and so on ...)

'Hai schmotka!' mirlotski momsk.
'Per dontcha hopni skipni truda wudsk!'
'Meem? Hopni skipni truda wudsk?
Ha! Ha! Ha! No! No! No!
(Aside.)
Heh! Heh! Heh!
(Aloud.)
Adios, momsk!'
(With his left hand, he imitates a skipping youth.)
Hopni, skipni, hopni, skipni, hopni, skipni truda wudsk.
(His tone becomes ominous.)
Meemskivai – omby odderzeiden der foretz, mirduschka – *Om*skivar!
(Deep, decadent, hungry voice.).
'Broizhni, broizhni! Broizhni, broizhni!'
Yach! Aglianastica, Omskivar. Das leetskicheelden ranski haidven Omski's inda vutz.
'Mir-*lo*,' Omski deech praznadya. *(Rubbing his stomach.)* 'Miro-*lo*! Porlo papno ob*scrod*nyi!
Das
(Imitating with his right hand a huge, slovenly beast crashing through the forest.)

broizhni, broizhni! Broizhni, broizhni!' Y
    byootsky dottsky?
Hai.
(Skipping in a semi-circle with his left hand.)
'Hopni, skipni, hopni, skipni, hopni, skipni – !'
*(Right hand, starting an opposite semi-circle toward the
same point.)*
'Broizhni, broizhni! Broizhni, broizhni – !'
(Left hand.)
'Hopni, skipni, hopni –. '
(Right hand.)
'Broizhni, broizhni –.'
(Left.)
'Hopni, skipni –.'
(Right.)
'Broizhni – .'
(The two hands confront each other.)
'Ah?'
*(As Marla, in a fearless – not to say foolhardy – falsetto,
chanting loudly.)*
'Irlo mirlo momsky meem! Eevno peevno
    pomsky *peem*!'
*(A moment – then the right hand, with a snort, gobbles the
left and remains alone. Charlie, with a shrug, tells the moral:)*
Blit?
(The others laugh and applaud.)

CATHERINE   Well, *Char*lie? You old *story*teller, you.

FROGGY   I don't believe it.

CHARLIE   Thank you.

ELLARD   Charlie, that was real *good*.

CHARLIE   Thank you.

BETTY	An' I understood practically all of it, I think.
CATHERINE	That's funny, I did too, I thought.
BETTY	That part about the tractor? That 'uz *real* clear, to me.
CATHERINE	Tractor?
CHARLIE	Hm?
BETTY	Wadn' there sump'm about a tractor, ridin' around?
CATHERINE	Oh, I don't know – .
CHARLIE	Trac-tor?
BETTY	Yeah.
CHARLIE	No.
CATHERINE	No, Betty, I didn't think so. There wadn' any tractor in the story.
CHARLIE	No. Story ees about – beeg machine – to cut ground.
ELLARD	'Big – .' Charlie, that *is*. That's a tractor.
CHARLIE	Oh?
ELLARD	Yes!
CHARLIE	Trac-tor! Oh!
ELLARD	Yes!
CHARLIE	Yes! *(To Betty.)* Yes. Story ees about – trac-tor.
BETTY	Ah!
CHARLIE	Yes!

BETTY	I thought I 'uz right about that.
CATHERINE	Well, my goodness.
CHARLIE	Yes. I am sorry.
BETTY	*No*, no, *no*.
CATHERINE	Don't be *sorry*.
CHARLIE	I am bad.
CATHERINE	No!
BETTY	Charlie!
CATHERINE	No, now, don't you even *say* that!
BETTY	Now, *no*, now? Charlie?
CATHERINE	That was a *won*derful story.
ELLARD	It *was*.
CATHERINE	It was *won*derful. You're – *you* – are wonderful. *You*. *(Charlie lowers his head.) Yes*!
CHARLIE	*(Sadly and adorably.)* No . . .
CATHERINE & BETTY	*Yes*!
CATHERINE	Yes, you *are*!
BETTY	You *are*!
CHARLIE	*(Looking up just a little.)* Oh . . .
CATHERINE	*(Hugging him, laughing.)* Oh, Charlie. Charlie.
BETTY	Look at him.
CATHERINE	My goodness.

BETTY	*Sweet?*
FROGGY	I'm gonna be sick in a minute.
BETTY	What?
FROGGY	Nothin'. Well. 'E's picked up a bit of English, I see.
BETTY	Oh, yes. Charlie's been in good hands, all right.
CHARLIE	Last night – I learn – to rid.
FROGGY	Ter 'rid'?
CHARLIE	To rid boook.
FROGGY	Ah!
CHARLIE	*(Referring to Ellard.)* He teach me.
FROGGY	Yes. *(To Ellard.)* And 'ow long did it take yer to teach 'im to, uh – ter 'rid'?
ELLARD	'Bout an hour.
FROGGY	One hour, eh?
CHARLIE	Yes! I show you. *(He brings a large volume down from the mantel.)*
CATHERINE	Well, how did I miss this?
CHARLIE	*(With the book open.)* You help.
ELLARD	'Kay.
CHARLIE	*(Reading.)* 'Shall I compare thee to a summer's day? Thou art more lovely – aa – ?' *(He points to a word.)*
ELLARD	*(Helping.)* 'And'?

CHARLIE   'And, more temperate.' *(To Ellard.)* Yes?

ELLARD   *(After studying the page another moment, and trying to conceal his astonishment at himself.)* Yeah. *(He looks at the page again.)*

CATHERINE   Well, Ellard? *(Ellard looks at her.)* All that's from just an hour?

ELLARD   Yeah.

CATHERINE   I can't be*lieve* that.

ELLARD   I know. Remember how long it took me to learn to read? 'Bout three years.

FROGGY   Wot d'yer think accounts for the difference?

ELLARD   I don't know. *(Not naming any names.)* I guess he just had a better teacher. *(And it's true, too.)*

FROGGY   *('I see.')* Ah!

CHARLIE   Yes. *(Speaking of Ellard.)* Remarkable.

CATHERINE   Well. I guess *so*, remarkable. Y'all are right. Pretty soon I'm gonna have to stop talkin' to you, Charlie.

CHARLIE   *(Pointing to her.)* Stop – talk? *(Points to himself.)*

CATHERINE   If you really know what I'm sayin', I can't tell you all my secrets, can I?

CHARLIE   I – I stop learn.

CATHERINE   *(Smiling.)* No, Charlie. *(Squeezing his shoulders.)* No. You go on and learn. Maybe I'll just tell you my secrets anyway.

CHARLIE   Yes?

CATHERINE	We'll see.
CHARLIE	Yes?
CATHERINE	We'll *see*.
CHARLIE	What mean – 'We'll see'?
CATHERINE	*(Giving in.)* Oh, it means, yes.
CHARLIE	*(Thoughtfully.)* 'We'll see.' Mean – yes.
CATHERINE	Yeah. This time it means yes.
CHARLIE	*(To Ellard.)* Een my contry, 'yes' ees – 'gok'.
ELLARD	Gok?
CHARLIE	Gok.
ELLARD	How do you say, 'no'?
CHARLIE	Blit.
ELLARD	*(Nods. Pause.)* Blit?
CHARLIE	Gok.
ELLARD	*(Absorbs this.)* Uh-huh.
CHARLIE	*(Offering tea.)* You – would like some?
ELLARD	*(Accepting it.)* Gok. *(Charlie nods. Catherine and Betty whisper and smile at Ellard, who affects not to notice. Ellard offers Charlie some tea.)* You?
CHARLIE	*(Accepting.)* We'll see. *(They sip happily. Froggy wheels away in disgust.)*
BETTY	*(To Froggy, beaming.)* Ain't this nice?
CHARLIE	Froe-gie? Ain't dees nice? *(He imitates Betty's pronunciation – 'nahse'.)*

FROGGY   *(Turning back.)* Very nice. Gettin' away wiv bloody murder, is wot it is.

BETTY   What?

FROGGY   No, nothin'. I feel a bit dull,[4] myself, but never mind.

BETTY   No, now, Frog. You can't help it if you ain't a foreigner.

FROGGY   No.

BETTY   Besides, we gotta make the most of Charlie. He's leavin' us tomorra'.

FROGGY   If we can get 'im ter go, yeh. *(Charlie smiles, sips.)*

CHARLIE   La, la. Blasny, blasny.

FROGGY   *(Under his breath.)* 'Blasny, blasny.' Right.

ELLARD   What's 'at mean? *(Charlie gestures to Froggy – 'Go ahead.')*

FROGGY   Wot, 'Blasny, blasny'? *(Squinting at Charlie.)* I might be wrong, but I think it means, 'Enjoy it while yer've got it.' Am I right, Charlie?

CHARLIE   *(The traitor.)* No. 'Blasny, blasny'? Eet mean – 'Ain't dees nice?'

FROGGY   Ah, yes. Well. Not far wrong, anyway, was I? *(Going to the door.)* Well – I'd like to stay, but I think I'd go mad. So – .

BETTY   *(Regretfully, standing.)* Oh . . .

---

[4] **dull**   in low spirits, 'down'

FROGGY   Be back tomorrow. *(To Catherine and Ellard.)* Nice
              to've met yer both. *(A last try.)* Charlie? 'Gomo
              rim jambo.'

CHARLIE   *(Who just can't help it.)* 'Gomo rim jambo'? *(He
              looks at the others, shrugs.)* 'I sleep with a pheas-
              ant'? *(This last line might be reinvented nightly by the
              actor playing Charlie.)*

FROGGY   *(With a smile of pure malice.)* Ohh, you –.

BETTY   *(At the window.)* Oh, look! It's David.

CATHERINE   *(Joining her.)* David? Well, about time. What's
              he doin' with that van?

ELLARD   Sellin' vegetables, maybe, from it?

BETTY   What?

ELLARD   Sellin' vegetables? Sometimes people sell
              vegetables from the backs of those.

BETTY   *(Looks at him for a long beat.)* Well – if you think
              so, then maybe that's right.

ELLARD   Yeah.

CATHERINE   Well, he's not gonna see me like this. You two
              keep him out there till I get back down.

BETTY and   All right. *(Betty and Ellard leave.)*
ELLARD

CATHERINE   Nice to meet you, Froggy.

FROGGY   Right. *(She exits. Froggy advances on Charlie.)*

CHARLIE   *(Immediately.)* I'm sorry! Something came over me.

FROGGY   Yeh, thanks a lot. Yer made me look like a
              bleedin' idiot.

CHARLIE   *(Groveling.)* I know, I – . *(Brightening.)* Well, I did, didn't I?

FROGGY   *Yeh!*

CHARLIE   I really did. And d'you know what? It wasn't that difficult.

FROGGY   Gor – !

CHARLIE   Nothing to it, really. That gives me an idea!

FROGGY   Oh, yeah? Well, I've got an idea – !

CHARLIE   Oh, Froggy, I'm sorry. I didn't mean to – . I – if only I could tell you what an adventure I've been having! I haven't quite sorted it out myself, yet, but I – Froggy, I think I'm acquiring a personality!

FROGGY   Oh?

CHARLIE   Yes! People here just seem to hand it to me piece by piece as they walk into the room! You see? You just did it too! I – suddenly I'm – a raconteur! And suddenly, I'm Catherine's confessor,[5] and I'm Ellard's prize pupil, and Betty's – pet skunk![6]

FROGGY   Her wot?

CHARLIE   Oh – . *(Ellard enters from outside. Charlie and Froggy go into doubletalk. Ellard picks up the volume of Shakespeare and goes up the stairs.)* And look. Look. Reading *Shake*speare! Because of *me*, you see? We – all

---

[5]**confessor**   a special person to whom you tell your secrets
[6]**pet skunk**   Betty had said earlier that she used to have a skunk which seemed to know what she was thinking, just as Charlie does

of us, we're becoming – we're making one another complete, and alive, and – oh, I can't explain. But – oh, I shall miss them. I shall miss them terribly.

FROGGY (*Softening a bit.*) Well – I suppose it's all right, then. I'm late. (*Starts off.*)

CHARLIE (*Stopping him.*) Froggy. Thank you. Thank you for making me a foreigner.

FROGGY I feel a bit like Doctor Frankenstein, but never mind. (*Breaks into a wry smile.*) 'Ave yourself a lark. (*He winks and is gone.*)

CHARLIE (*Pacing furiously.*) Frankenstein. Yes . . .

Further reading

Read the rest of the play to find out what happens to Charlie and how he manages to save the family from a very unpleasant plot. Another hilarious play in which a man pretends to be someone else (in this case a middle-aged woman!) is *Charley's Aunt*, written in 1892 by Brandon Thomas.

Activities

Lad Carl

Before you read

1   As a class, discuss stories in which one character defeats another by playing a clever trick.

What's it about?

2   In small groups, make a list of Carl's qualities, divided into 'good qualities' and 'bad qualities'. Discuss which of them (for example, cleverness) can be used for both good and bad ends.

3   In groups of four, create the front page of the day's newspaper which follows the raid.
   ● One person writes a full account of what happened, starting with the moment when the villagers received a message from Carl carried by his pet pigeon.
   ● Another writes up an interview with Carl, following the defeat of the gang.
   ● The third writes a feature on Carl, based on interviews with his mother, Hallbjorn the farmer, Agnar the old caretaker and any other villagers.
   ● The fourth has managed to get some time in prison with Thorgaut and reports his feelings about what happened.

Thinking about the text

4   Imagine you are Thorgaut. What exactly is bothering you in Scene 9? Write a paragraph on your thoughts as you leave the cabin.

5   At the end of the play, three of the gang lie dead. Hold a class discussion in which you give your opinions on Carl's methods for catching the thieves. Should he be praised or criticised?

Arguments for Carl include:
   ● the thieves were dangerous law-breakers
   ● most of them were willing to kill Agnar, the old caretaker

Arguments against Carl include:
   ● he gained the gang's trust and then betrayed them
   ● the men were gunned down mercilessly – they should have been arrested to face a proper trial

The Wind in the Willows

Before you read

1   As a class, talk about the many stories you have read or films you have seen, featuring talking animals. You might know George Orwell's *Animal Farm*, for example. In these stories, how far do the characters look and behave like animals, and how far like humans?

What's it about?

2   Toad is one of the four main characters in the story and many people's favourite. This is perhaps because, in keeping with most people, he has both good and bad qualities.

   a   In small groups, re-read the extract, and make a note of the things Toad says and does.

      Make one list of examples which show him to be:
- charming
- funny
- bold

      and another list of examples which show him to be:
- conceited
- ignorant of how ordinary people live
- ungrateful.

   b   Then perform the extract. Take it in turns to play Toad, bringing out his good and bad qualities.

3   Still in your groups, talk about the way Toad and Albert are presented here. How far do they talk and behave as animals, and how far as humans? Compare the ways in which:
- the Bargewoman treats Toad when she first meets him, with her reactions when she realises who he is
- Albert is presented, with the way Toad treats him.

Thinking about the text

4   The original National Theatre production had a very elaborate set which permitted a realistic train and barge to appear. Parts of the stage also revolved to represent different places, such as the prison and canal bank. Imagine you were staging a school production of this play. Decide in groups how you could represent the train and barge, and the different locations, in a much simpler way.

Blackadder: Potato

Before you read

1   There were four series of Blackadder and it has been voted one of Britain's favourite television comedies. Make a list of your own favourite TV comedies (not including Blackadder) and write a sentence on each one stating what it is about it that you find particularly funny. For example, do you laugh most at the characters, the dialogue, the situations they find themselves in, or a combination of several things? What, in your opinion, has been the funniest television comedy series that you have seen?

What's it about?

2   Much of the humour in Blackadder derives from the fact that the characters are such different types. Make a list of quotations from the extract which illustrate:
   • Baldrick's stupidity
   • Lord Percy's cowardice
   • Blackadder's cunning.

3   The real Queen Elizabeth the First was a brilliant and well-educated woman, but it is also true that she expected to be flattered and could be harsh with people who displeased her. Consult an online encyclopedia to find out more about her. How would you describe the Queen in Blackadder?

   Look, for example, at the moments when she:
   • is seen throwing rings at Raleigh's dunce's cap
   • greets Edmund, Percy and Baldrick
   • reacts to Edmund's reference to 'wedding bells'
   • talks about Raleigh's postponed execution
   • demands presents
   • asks Melchett for a death warrant
   • changes her reaction to the boomerang.

   Use these examples to write a short entry for an online encyclopedia on 'Queen Elizabeth the First in Blackadder'.

Thinking about the text

4   When you write a television screenplay the stage directions are extremely important. Pick three from the extract and draw a sketch for each to show what the moment looks like. Interesting examples include:

  ● (*They look around the room. The trunk the sheet came from is standing invitingly wide open*)

  ● (*. . . we see a very disgruntled Raleigh wearing a dunce's outfit, with the Queen throwing rings at his cap, and Melchett and Nursie looking on*)

  ● (*The boomerang comes back and hits Percy on the head, knocking him down. The Queen changes her mind on the stick*)

5   Write a scene in which Blackadder, Percy, Baldrick, the Queen and Nursie meet Shakespeare. Perhaps Edmund is fed up with the Queen gushing over Shakespeare's plays and unwisely boasts that he could write one . . .

The Foreigner

Before you read

1   Talk with a partner about times when you felt shy or embarrassed
and unwilling to talk to people. Where were you? What happened?
How did you deal with the situation?

What's it about?

2   It has often been said that the way we are has a lot to do with the
way people treat us; and that we can change if we are treated differently. For example, if you tell someone they are a no-hoper, they
might fulfil your expectations and achieve nothing; if you praise
them, and take an interest, they might have the confidence to do
well.

When have you seen this happen? As a class, talk about examples
from school or your life outside school. Then discuss how it is
shown in the extract. What has happened to help:
  ● Ellard to stop thinking of himself as stupid
  ● Betty to feel that she isn't old and useless
  ● Charlie to stop believing that he is boring, and find out that he
    has a personality?

3   Charlie's tale in his 'foreign' tongue can be very funny on stage. In
pairs rehearse a performance of it. One person acts Charlie's lines
while the other person offers advice on how to say them. Then
swap roles.
  ● First talk over what happens in Charlie's story – it is particularly
    important to understand what happens at the end!
  ● Notice that some of Charlie's 'foreign language' is amusingly
    like English: practise saying the following to make sure the
    audience can hear the similarities:
    'Ah! Byootsky dottsky!'
    'Meem? Hopni skipni truda woodsk?'
    'Adios, momsk!'
  ● Make sure that you have a different voice for the old woman,
    her daughter Marla and the hungry beast.
  ● It will help to follow the stage directions very carefully.

Some of them tell you how to speak a line: (*His tone becomes ominous*).

Some tell you which actions should accompany a line: (*Rubbing his stomach*).

Some give you the chance to make up movements of your own: (*With appropriate gestures*).

Thinking about the text

4　For *The Foreigner* to work on stage, all the actors have to speak in a distinctive accent which is an important part of their personality. Froggy is a Londoner, Charlie speaks with a fake foreign accent, Betty, Ellard and Catherine are all from the southern states of America.

In groups of four, re-read the extract. Talk about the way the spelling helps you to 'hear' the characters' pronunciation. It will help to repeat some of the words and phrases aloud to one another; for example:
- Ellard's 'Lay-ump'
- Betty's 'Wadn' there sump'm about a tractor, ridin' around?'
- Froggy's ''At's right, Charlie . . . 'Ow's it goin', then?'.

Make up a foreign accent that fits Charlie's invented language. Then act out the first two pages of the script, bringing out each character's accent and personality.

5　Choose a well-known folk tale or nursery rhyme, or a famous story such as *Dracula* or *Frankenstein*. Draft a script for a short retelling of it in a made-up 'foreign' language like Charlie's and include some stage directions to remind you how to say the lines and which gestures should accompany them.
- The new version should sound foreign but include enough clues to enable audiences to work out what the story is.
- Remember that much of the fun in Charlie's story came from the different characters' voices.

When you have written a first draft, perform the story for a partner. Discuss improvements, redraft, and perform it again.

Finally, as a class, listen to other people's 'foreign tales'.

Compare and contrast

1 All of these extracts feature characters who deceive others. In small groups, talk about deception. Using the events of these plays as evidence, when is it right to deceive others? What can be gained by choosing to deceive others rather than being open and honest with them?

2 Pick two of these plays and jot down some examples of humour. Look at:
   - the dialogue
   - the characters
   - the plot.

   Find examples where the comedy is used for a serious purpose. Which is the funniest extract, in your opinion?

3 Working in pairs, decide which of the three stage plays – *Lad Carl*, *The Wind in the Willows* and *The Foreigner* – would make the best film. Then pick one scene from your chosen play and redraft it as a screenplay. As you write, imagine what you want the film audience to see and include descriptions in your directions. Here is an example from *The Elephant Man*:

   Through the high barred window, we see the dark sky. Merrick is on his bed in his sleeping posture. A dim gaslight burns in the room.

4 When a play is performed the director and designer have to think carefully about how the characters should look. Pick one character from each of *Lad Carl*, *The Wind in the Willows* and *The Foreigner* (avoid *Blackadder* which you will probably have seen already on television) and draw a sketch that shows what they look like and what costume they should wear. Don't worry if you are not a great artist: add notes around the drawings to explain your ideas. Under each drawing write a short paragraph explaining why you have chosen the particular costume.

4 Laughter

Comedy, whether on stage or screen, takes many forms; and, as has often been said, a sense of humour is a personal thing. So you might find some of the following extracts funnier than others. But they are examples of the ways in which, throughout the ages, human beings have stayed sane by laughing at themselves.

Activities

1   What makes you laugh? In groups, tell each other the funniest moment you have ever seen on stage, film or television. What in particular made you laugh? Think about:
    - the way the situation had been set up
    - what the characters said
    - what they did
    - the skill of the actors.

2   There are many different kinds of comedy and often several kinds will appear in the same comic moment. In pairs, try to write a definition of each of the following kinds of comedy, with an example for each one:
    - satire
    - parody
    - farce
    - situation comedy
    - irony
    - black comedy
    - comedy of manners
    - romantic comedy
    - verbal comedy
    - physical comedy.

To get you started, use a video library or the internet to find the following sketches from the BBC: *Two Ronnies: 'fork handles'* (as an example of verbal comedy); and *Best moment in Only Fools and Horses* (as an example of physical comedy).

3   It is difficult to list the ingredients of comedy, but many great comic moments include one or more of the following:

- surprise
- incongruity (something that doesn't seem to fit in or is inappropriate to the situation)
- people being forced together and unable to escape (such as a family or group of workmates).

Write a short comic sketch that includes at least one of these ingredients.

Wyrd Sisters

by Terry Pratchett, adapted for the stage by Stephen Briggs

Wyrd Sisters is a comedy based very loosely on Shakespeare's *Macbeth*. The 'Sisters' of the title are three witches: Granny Weatherwax, Nanny Ogg and Magrat Garlick. In this first scene, they decide to call up a demon to find out about the strange goings-on in the kingdom, such as the disappearance of their cat Greebo.

The wicked Duke Felmet (who has come to power by murdering King Verence) suspects that the witches know something. Assisted by his nasty wife the Duchess, he imprisons Nanny Ogg and they plan to torture her for information.

Scene 7

Nanny is on stage. Granny and Magrat enter.

NANNY He's disappeared, old Greebo. Haven't seen him for a couple of days. *(a new thought)* Here, what about that earthquake, then?

GRANNY Extremely worrying developments of a magical tendency are even now afoot.

NANNY Well, we'd better have a look, then. *(she takes the lid off her wash copper[1])* I think perhaps we should join hands. Is the door shut?

(Magrat nods)

GRANNY What are you going to try?

NANNY I always say you can't go wrong with a good Invocation.[2] Haven't done one for years.

---

[1]**copper**   huge tub for boiling water
[2]**Invocation**   spell for calling up a spirit

MAGRAT   Oh, but you can't. Not here. You need a cauldron, and a magic sword. And an octogram.[3] And spices, all sorts of stuff.

(Nanny and Granny exchange glances)

GRANNY   It's not her fault. It's all them grimmers she bought.

MAGRAT   Grimoires.[4]

GRANNY   You don't need none of that. You just use whatever you've got. *(she picks up a rolling pin, holds it aloft and declaims)* We conjure and abjure[5] thee by means of this . . . weighty and terrible rolling pin.

---

[3]**octogram**   eight-sided star to protect you while casting spells
[4]**Grimoires**   textbooks of magic
[5]**abjure**   reject, disbelieve in *(she probably doesn't know what it means)*

MAGRAT   *(picking up a packet of soap flakes)* See how we scatter *(she sighs)* rather old washing soda and some extremely hard soap flakes in thy honour. Really, Nanny, I don't think –

NANNY   And I invoke[6] and bind thee with the balding scrubbing brush of Art and the washboard of Protection.

MAGRAT   Honesty is all very well, but somehow it just isn't the same.

GRANNY   You listen to me, girl. Demons don't care about the outward shape of things. It's what you think that matters. Get on with it.

   (They all look, in deepest concentration, at the copper. Smoke rises from it, and a head appears)

DEMON   Well?

GRANNY   Who're you?

DEMON   My name is unpronounceable in your tongue, woman.

GRANNY   I'll be the judge of that. And don't you call me woman.

DEMON   Very well. My name is WxrtHlt-jwlpklz.

NANNY   Where were you when the vowels were handed out? Behind the door?

GRANNY   Well, Mr . . . WxrtHlt-jwlpklz *(it's a good effort, and pretty close to the Demon's pronunciation)*, I expect you're wondering why we called you here tonight.

---

[6]**invoke**   call up

DEMON	You're not supposed to say that. You're supposed to say –
GRANNY	Shut up. We have the sword of Art and the octogram of Protection, I warn you.
DEMON	They look like a balding scrubbing brush and a washboard to me. You are allowed three questions.
GRANNY	*(to the others)* We must be careful; Demons always tell the truth, but only as much as they need to. We must phrase our questions very carefully. *(to the Demon)* Is there something strange at large in the kingdom?
DEMON	You mean stranger than usual? No. There is nothing strange.
GRANNY	Hold on, hold on. *(she tries again)* Is there something in the kingdom that wasn't there before?
DEMON	No.
GRANNY	*(a last try)* What the hell's going on? And no mucking about trying to wriggle out of it, otherwise I'll boil you.
	(The Demon hesitates at this new approach)
	Magrat, just bring over that kindling, will you?
DEMON	I protest at this treatment.
GRANNY	Yes, well. I haven't got time to bandy legs[7] with you all night. These word games might be all very well for wizards, but we've other fish to fry.

---

[7] **bandy legs**   the expression is usually 'bandy words' (to argue); here, 'bandy' means bent outwards

NANNY	Or boil.
DEMON	(*a little worried now*) Look, we're not supposed to volunteer[8] information just like that. There are rules, you know.
NANNY	There's some old oil in the can in the shed, Magrat.
DEMON	If I simply tell you . . .
GRANNY	(*encouragingly*) Yes?
DEMON	You won't let on, will you?
GRANNY	Not a word.
MAGRAT	Lips are sealed.
DEMON	There is nothing new in the Kingdom, but the land has woken up.
GRANNY	What do you mean?
DEMON	It's unhappy. It wants a king that cares for it.
GRANNY	You don't mean the people, do you?
	(*Demon shakes its head*)
	No, I didn't think so.
NANNY	What – ?
	(*Granny holds up a hand*)
GRANNY	Can you tell us why?
DEMON	I'm just a demon. What do I know? Only what it is, not the why and how of it.
GRANNY	I see.

[8]**volunteer**   give without being forced

DEMON	May I go now?
GRANNY	Mmm?
DEMON	Please?
GRANNY	Oh. Yes. Run along. Thank you.
DEMON	*(after a pause)* You wouldn't mind banishing me,[9] would you?
GRANNY	*(still distracted)* What?
DEMON	Only I'd feel better if I was properly banished. 'Run along' lacks that certain something.
GRANNY	Oh, well. If it gives you pleasure. Magrat! Do the honours, will you?
MAGRAT	Certainly. Right. Okay. Um. Begone, foul fiend, unto the blackest pit . . .
	(The head starts to sink back into the copper. As it goes . . .)
DEMON	Run aaaalonggg . . .
NANNY	Well. I wonder if that's why Greebo's vanished.
GRANNY	Cats can look after themselves. Countries can't. Duke Felmet hates the kingdom. The villagers say that when they go to see him he just stares at them and giggles and rubs his hands and twitches.
NANNY	The old king used to shout at them and kick them out of the castle. But he was always very gracious about it. You felt he meant it. People like to feel they're valued.

---

[9]**banishing me**   sending me away formally – demons are supposed to be
banished rather than 'let go'

GRANNY	The kingdom is worried. You heard what the demon said. This morning when I opened my door, there were all the animals of the forest, just stood outside.
MAGRAT	What did they say?
GRANNY	Nothing. Animals, aren't they? Knew what they wanted, though. Rid of the king. They was sent, by the kingdom, the land itself. It doesn't care if people are good or bad. But it expects the king to care for it.
MAGRAT	It's a bit like a dog, really. A dog doesn't care if its master's good or bad, just so long as it likes the dog.
NANNY	What are we going to do about it?
GRANNY	Nothing. You know we can't meddle. *(Pause)*
MAGRAT	You know the Fool, who lives up at the castle?
NANNY	Little man with runny eyes?
MAGRAT	Not that little. What's his name, do you happen to know?
GRANNY	He's just called Fool. No job for a man, that. Running around with bells on.
NANNY	His mother was a Beldame,[10] from over Blackglass way. Bit of a beauty when she was younger. Broke many a heart, she did. Bit of a scandal there, I did hear. Think he was named after his master the king. Verence. Granny's

---

[10]**Beldame**   witch

right, though. At the end of the day, a Fool's a
Fool.

GRANNY   Why d'you want to know, Magrat?

MAGRAT   (blushing) Oh . . . one of the girls in the village
was asking me.

(Nanny clears her throat, and nudges Granny)

NANNY   It's a steady job. I'll grant you that.

GRANNY   Huh. A man who tinkles all day. No kind of a
husband for anyone, I'd say.

NANNY   You . . . she'd always know where he was.
You'd just have to listen.

GRANNY   Never trust a man with horns on his hat.

MAGRAT   (suddenly) You're a pair of silly old women. And
I'm going home! (she stalks out)

GRANNY   Well!
and NANNY

(Lights out)

Scene 8   The Castle Dungeon

Noise of echoey dripping water. Nanny, the Duke and Duchess are on stage.
Also on stage is King Verence (in a green follow-spot[11]), sitting in a corner
and watching the action. Nanny is in the stocks. The Duke's hands are now
a bit bloody, and he is working away at them using a rather rusty-looking
rasp.

DUKE   Quite comfortable, are we?

NANNY   Apart from these stocks, you mean?

---

[11]**follow-spot**   stage light that follows the actor wherever he or she goes

DUKE   I am impervious to your foul blandishments.[12] I scorn your devious wiles.[13] You are to be tortured, I'll have you know.

DUCHESS   *(since that seems to have had no effect)* And then you will be burned.

NANNY   Okay.

DUKE   Okay?

NANNY   Well, it's freezing down here. What's that big wardrobe thing with the spikes?

DUKE   Aha. Now you realise, do you? That, my dear lady, is the Iron Maiden.[14] It's the latest thing. Well may you . . .

NANNY   Can I have a go in it?

DUKE   Your pleas fall on deaf . . . what?

DUCHESS   This insouciance[15] gives you pleasure, but soon you'll laugh on the other side of your face!

NANNY   It's only got this side.

DUCHESS   *(fingering a pair of pliers)* We shall see.

DUKE   And you need not think any others of your people will come to your aid. We alone hold the keys of this dungeon. Ha ha. You will be an example to all those who have been spreading malicious[16] rumours about me. I hear the voices all the time, lying . . .

---

[12]**blandishments**   flattery used to get round someone
[13]**devious wiles**   underhand trickery
[14]**Iron Maiden**   instrument of torture in which people are crushed by spikes
[15]**insouciance**   cheerful lack of worry; a devil-may-care attitude
[16]**malicious**   spiteful, aimed at doing harm

DUCHESS   Enough! Come, Leonal. We will let her reflect on her fate for a while.

DUKE   *(muttering, as he exits)* . . . the faces . . . wicked lies . . . I wasn't there, and anyway he fell . . .
(Duke and Duchess exit. A moment's silence)

NANNY   All right. I can see you. Who are you?
(King Verence steps forward)

I saw you making faces behind him. All I could do to keep a straight face.

VERENCE   I wasn't making faces, woman. I was scowling.

NANNY   'Ere, I know you. You're dead. You're the late King Verence.

VERENCE   I prefer the term 'passed over'. I'm afraid it was I who borrowed your cat: I knew you'd come looking for it.

NANNY   What's that big bed thing over there?

VERENCE   The rack.[17]

NANNY   Oh. I suppose you're no good at locks?

VERENCE   *(shaking his head)* But surely, to a witch this is all so much . . .

NANNY   Solid iron. You might be able to walk through it, but I can't.

VERENCE   I didn't realise. I thought witches could do magic.

NANNY   Young man, you will oblige me by shutting up!

---

[17]**the rack**   another instrument of torture on which people are painfully stretched

VERENCE	Madam! I am a king!
NANNY	You are also dead, so I wouldn't aspire[18] to hold any opinions if I was you.
	(Pause. Lights go down and up to indicate the passage of time. During the brief blackout a clock chimes)
	I spy, with my little eye, something beginning with P.
VERENCE	Oh. Er, Pliers.
NANNY	No.
VERENCE	Pilliwinks?
NANNY	That's a pretty name. What's that?
VERENCE	It's a kind of thumbscrew.
NANNY	No.
VERENCE	Choke-pear?[19]
NANNY	That's a C, and anyway I don't know what it is. You're a bit too good at these names. You sure you didn't use them when you were alive?
VERENCE	Absolutely, Nanny.
NANNY	Boys that tell lies go to a bad place.
VERENCE	Lady Felmet had most of them installed herself. It's the truth.
NANNY	All right. It was 'pinchers'.

---

[18]**aspire**   have ambitions
[19]**Choke-pear**   iron 'pear' placed in the mouth from which spokes would
   spring out in all directions

VERENCE   But that's just another name for pliers. *(pause)* They'll be back soon. Are you sure you'll be all right?

NANNY   If I'm not, how much help can you be?

(A sound of bolts sliding back. The Duke, Duchess and Fool enter)

DUCHESS   We will begin with the Showing of the Implements.

NANNY   Seen 'em. Leastways all the ones beginning with P, S, I, T and W.

DUCHESS   Then let us see how long you can keep that light conversational tone.

NANNY   Is this going to take long? I haven't had breakfast.

DUCHESS   Now, woman, will you confess?

NANNY   What to?

DUCHESS   It's common knowledge. Treason. Malicious witchcraft. Harbouring[20] the king's enemies. Theft of the crown and spreading false rumours.

NANNY   What false rumours?

DUKE   *(hoarsely)* Concerning the accidental death of the late King Verence.

NANNY   Oh, I don't know nothing false.

(Verence whispers to her, telling her what happened)

I know you stabbed him, and you gave him the dagger. It was at the top of the stairs.

---

[20]**Harbouring**   sheltering, hiding

Just by the suit of armour with the pike.[21] And you said, 'If it's to be done, it's better if it's done quickly'[22] or something, and then you snatched the king's own dagger . . .

DUKE   You lie! There were no witnesses. We made . . . there was nothing to witness! I heard someone in the dark, but there was no-one there!

DUCHESS   Do shut up, Leonal!

DUKE   Who told her? Did you tell her?

DUCHESS   And calm down. No-one told her. She's a witch, for goodness sake, they find out about these things. Second glance, or something.

NANNY   Sight.

DUCHESS   Which you will not possess much longer, my good woman, unless you tell us who else knows and indeed assist us on a number of other matters. *(pause)* And now we will commence. Your friends can't help you now.

(Lights out)

Further reading

If you have enjoyed the humour in this extract, you should try more Terry Pratchett. He has written numerous books, including the popular comic fantasy *Discworld* series. *Wyrd Sisters* is his and Stephen Briggs' comic version of Shakespeare's *Macbeth*. You could read Shakespeare's play to see how it has been adapted.

---

[21]**pike**   long-handled weapon with a metal point
[22]**'If it's to be done . . .'**   a misquotation of Macbeth's speech (Act 1 Scene 7 line 1) when he is thinking about killing the King

Fawlty Towers: A Touch of Class
by John Cleese and Connie Booth

This extract is from the very first episode of the television comedy series *Fawlty Towers*. Set in a small seaside hotel, it features Basil Fawlty, the hotel-owner, Sybil, his wife, Polly, the general help, and Manuel, the Spanish waiter.

In this episode, Basil is, as usual, extremely stressed. Sybil has asked him to hang a picture, make up the bill for some departing guests and type up the day's menu, but there seems to be one interruption after another . . .

The reception bell rings. Basil goes to the reception desk; standing there is a very non-aristocratic-looking[1] cockney, Danny Brown.

DANNY	'Allo! *(Basil stands appalled)* Got a room?
BASIL	. . . I beg your pardon?
DANNY	Got a room for tonight, mate?
BASIL	. . . I shall have to see, sir . . . single?
DANNY	Yeah. No, make it a double, I feel lucky today! *(smiling appreciatively at Polly, who is passing)* 'Allo . . .
POLLY	*(smiling nicely)* Good morning.
	Danny watches her as she leaves. He turns back to Basil who is staring at him with loathing.
DANNY	Only joking.
BASIL	No we haven't.
DANNY	What?
BASIL	No we haven't any rooms. Good day . . .

---

[1] **non-aristocratic-looking**   the kind of person Basil would describe as 'common'

SYBIL   *(coming in)* Number seven is free, Basil.

BASIL   What? . . . oh . . . Mr Tone is in number seven,
             dear.

SYBIL   No, he left while you were putting the picture
             up, Basil . . . *(to Danny)* You have luggage, sir?

DANNY   Just one case. *(to Basil, pointedly)* In the car . . .
             the white sports.

             Basil closes his eyes in agony. Sybil rings the bell.

SYBIL   Fill this in, would you, sir?

BASIL   *(quietly)* If you can.

SYBIL   I hope you enjoy your stay *(looking at register)*,
             Mr Brown.

             Manuel arrives.

BASIL   *(slowly)* Er, Manuel, would you fetch this
             gentleman's case from the car outside. Take
             it to room seven.

MANUEL   . . . is not easy for me.

BASIL   What?

MANUEL   Is not easy for me . . . *entender.*[2]

BASIL   Ah! It's not easy for you to understand.
             Manuel . . . *(to Danny)* We're training him . . .
             he's from Barcelona . . . in Spain. *(to Manuel)*
             Obtener[3] *la valisa* . . .

MANUEL   *Qué?*[4]

---

[2]*entender*   to understand
[3]*Obtener* . . .   Basil's Spanish is not very good; he is trying to say: 'Take the
    case in the white sports car to room seven, please. Quickly.'
[4]*Qué?*   What?

BASIL   *La valisa en el,* er, *auto bianco sportiv . . . y . . . a la sala . . . siete . . . por favor. Pronto.*

MANUEL   Is impossible!

BASIL   What?

MANUEL   Is impossible.

BASIL   Look, it's perfectly simple!

DANNY   *(fluently)* Manuel – *sirvase buscar mi equipaje que esta en el automovil blanco y lo traer a la sala numero siete.*

MANUEL   *Señor habla Español!*

DANNY   *Solo un poco, lo siento. Pero he olvidado mucho.*

MANUEL   *No, no, habla muy bien. Muy muy bien. Formidable!*

DANNY   *Gracias, gracias.*

MANUEL   *Lo voy a coger ahora.*[5] *(runs off to get the case)*

BASIL   . . . Well, if there's anything else, I'm sure Manuel will be able to tell you . . . as you seem to get on so well together. *(goes into the office)*

DANNY   *(calling after him)* Key?

         Basil comes back, takes the key from the hook and slams it down on the desk. Returning to the office he sits down, and switches on a cassette of Brahms.[6] *He settles back in rapture, but hears Sybil coming and rushes back to the picture in the lobby.*

---

[5]***sirvase buscar . . .***   'please fetch my luggage which is in the white car and take it to room number seven.' 'The gentleman speaks Spanish!' 'Only a little, I'm afraid. But it's very rusty.' 'No, no, you speak it very well. Very, very well. Excellent!' 'Thank you, thank you.' 'I'm going to get it straightaway.'
[6]***Brahms***   Basil's favourite classical composer

BASIL Hallo dear . . . just doing the picture.

SYBIL Don't forget the menu.

BASIL . . . I beg your pardon?

SYBIL Don't forget the menu.

BASIL I thought you said you wanted . . . Right! *(puts the picture down)* I'll do the menu.

SYBIL You could have had them both done by now if you hadn't spent the whole morning skulking in there listening to that racket. *(goes out)*

BASIL Racket? That's **Brahms**! Brahms's Third Racket!! . . . *(to himself)* The whole morning! . . . I had two bars.

In the dining room, Polly is taking Danny's order.

POLLY Ready to order?

DANNY Er, yeah. What's a gralefrit?

POLLY Grapefruit.

DANNY And creme pot . . . pot rouge?

POLLY Portuguese. Tomato soup.

DANNY I'll have the gralefrit. Now – balm carousel . . . lamb?

POLLY Casserole.

DANNY Sounds good. Does it come with a smile?

POLLY It comes with sprouts or carrots.

DANNY Oh, smile's extra, is it?

POLLY You'll get one if you eat up all your sprouts. *(exits)*

DANNY   *(half registering a figure on the other side of the room)*
Waiter!

     Basil freezes and then comes balefully[7] towards Danny.

BASIL   . . . I beg your pardon?

DANNY   Oh, 'allo. Can I have some wine please?

BASIL   The waiter is busy, sir, but I will bring you the
carte des vins[8] when I have finished attending
to this gentleman. *(indicates the table he has just
left)*

DANNY   Oh, fine – no hurry.

BASIL   *(muttering on his way to the other table)* Oh, good,
how nice, how very thoughtful . . . *(at the other
table)* I trust the beer is to your satisfaction, sir?

MR WATSON   . . . Yes, fine.

BASIL   Ah, good. May I wish you *bon appétit. (snaps his
fingers)* Manuel! *(Manuel runs in)* Would you
fetch the wine list, please?

MANUEL   *(not moving) Si, señor.*

BASIL   . . . The wine list. The wine . . . *vino. (Manuel
starts to move)* No, no. The list! There, there, the
list! *(points to it – it is on another table)* The list,
there! The red . . . **there!** . . . There!!

     *He picks up the list, hands it to Manuel, then gets Manuel
to hand it to him so that he can give it to Danny.*

DANNY   'Ave you got a half bottle of the Beaujolais?[9]

---

[7]***balefully***   menacingly, threateningly
[8]***carte des vins***   wine list
[9]**Beaujolais**   a French wine

BASIL   Yes.

DANNY   Oh, fine.

Basil withdraws the wine list with a flourish, knocking the grapefruit out of Polly's hand as she approaches the table.

BASIL   Right! Never mind! Never mind! Manuel – another grapefruit for table twelve please . . . Manuel! *(pointing at the grapefruit on the floor – to other guests)* I do beg your pardon . . . I'm so sorry . . .

Manuel picks up the grapefruit and cleans it. He is about to replace it on the table.

BASIL   . . . No! . . . Throw it away.

MANUEL   *Qué?*

BASIL   Throw . . . it . . . away!

MANUEL   Throw . . . it . . . away?

BASIL   *(miming a throw)* Throw it away!! Now!!!

Manuel throws it away; it lands on another table. Basil retrieves it, grabs Manuel, and runs with him out of the room.

BASIL   *(to the other tables as he passes)* Sorry! . . . Sorry! . . . Sorry!

They disappear into the kitchen. There is the sound of a slap and a yelp from Manuel. Polly appears bearing Danny's grapefruit.

POLLY   Sorry about that.

DANNY   No, I like a bit of cabaret.[10] *(picks up Polly's sketch pad from the table)* You left your sketch.

POLLY   Oh! Sorry.

---

[10]**cabaret**   entertainment, usually in a bar or restaurant

DANNY It's very good. Do you sell any?

POLLY Enough to keep me in waitressing. *(she leaves as Basil reappears with the Beaujolais)*

BASIL One **half** bottle of Beaujolais. *(he is about to open the bottle when the reception bell rings)* . . . Sybil!

SYBIL *(popping her head round the door)* Someone at reception, dear. *(she vanishes)*

(Basil hurries bad-temperedly into the lobby. Melbury is standing there.)

BASIL Yes, yes, well, yes?

MELBURY . . . Er, well, I was wondering if you could offer me accommodation for a few nights?

BASIL *(very cross)* Well, have you booked?

MELBURY . . . I'm sorry?

BASIL Have you booked, have you booked?

MELBURY No.

BASIL *(to himself)* Oh dear!

MELBURY Why, are you full?

BASIL Oh, we're not full . . . we're not **full** . . . of course we're not **full**!!

MELBURY I'd like, er . . .

BASIL One moment, one moment, please . . . yes?

MELBURY A single room with a . . .

BASIL Your **name**, please, could I have your name?

MELBURY	Melbury.

The phone rings; Basil picks it up.

BASIL	*(to Melbury)* One second please. *(to phone)* Hello? . . . Ah, yes, Mr O'Reilly,[11] well it's perfectly simple. When I asked you to build me a wall I was rather hoping that instead of just dumping the bricks in a pile you might have found time to cement them together . . . you know, one on top of another, in the traditional fashion. *(to Melbury, testily)* Could you fill it in, please? *(to phone)* Oh, splendid! Ah, yes, but **when,** Mr O'Reilly? *(to Melbury, who is having difficulty with the register)* there – there!! *(to phone)* Yes, but when? Yes, yes . . . ah! . . . the flu! *(to Melbury)* Both names, please. *(to phone)* Yes, I should have guessed, Mr O'Reilly, that and the potato famine[12] I suppose . . .

MELBURY	I beg your pardon?

BASIL	Would you put **both** your names, please? . . . *(to phone)* Well, will you give me a **date?**

MELBURY	Er . . . I only use one.

BASIL	*(with a withering look)* You don't have a first name?

MELBURY	No, I am **Lord** Melbury, so I simply sign myself[13] 'Melbury'.

There is a long, long pause.

---

[11]**Mr O'Reilly**   a local Irish builder who has been promising to build a wall in the hotel but keeps failing to turn up

[12]**potato famine**   widespread starvation which hit Ireland in the mid-19th century

[13]**I simply sign myself . . .**   Lords often sign with just their one-word title

BASIL   *(to phone)* Go away. *(puts phone down)* . . . I'm **so** sorry to have kept you waiting, your lordship . . . I **do** apologize, **please** forgive me. Now, was there something, is there something, anything, I can do for you? Anything at all?

MELBURY   Well, I have filled this in . . .

BASIL   Oh, please don't bother with that. *(he takes the form and throws it away)* Now, a special room? . . . a single? A double? A suite? . . . Well, we don't have any suites, but we do have some beautiful doubles with a view . . .

MELBURY   No, no, just a single.

BASIL   Just a single! Absolutely! How very wise if I may say so, your honour.

MELBURY   With a bath.

BASIL   Naturally, naturally! *Naturellement!*[14] *(he roars with laughter)*

MELBURY   I shall be staying for one or two nights . . .

BASIL   Oh please! Please! . . . Manuel!! *(he bangs the bell; nothing happens)* . . . Well, it's . . . it's rather grey today, isn't it?

MELBURY   Oh, yes, it is, rather.

BASIL   Of course usually down here it's quite beautiful, but today is a real old . . . er . . . rotter. *(another bang on the bell)* Manuel!!! . . . Still . . . it's good for the wheat.

---

[14]***Naturellement!*** Basil thinks it is smart to add the occasional word of
French

MELBURY	Yes, er, I suppose so.

BASIL Oh yes! I hear it's coming along wonderfully at the moment! Thank God! I love the wheat . . . there's no sight like a field of wheat waving in the . . . waving in . . . Manuel!!!! *(he bangs the bell as hard as he can; no result)* . . . Well, how are you? I mean, if it's not a personal question. Well, it **is** a personal . . . *(he dashes from behind the desk)* Let me get your cases for you, please allow me . . .

MELBURY . . . Oh, thank you very much, they're just outside.

BASIL Splendid. Thank you so much. I won't be one moment . . .

He sprints off, collects the cases, and returns to find Sybil talking to Lord Melbury at the counter.

BASIL . . . Ah, Lord Melbury. May I introduce my wife?

MELBURY Yes, we have met.

BASIL My wife, may I introduce your lordship.

SYBIL Thank you, Basil, we've sorted it out.

BASIL Splendid, splendid.

MELBURY I wonder, could I deposit this case with you . . . it's just a few valuables?

BASIL Valuable, of course. Please let me take it now. I'll put it in the safe straight away. Sybil, would you put this in the safe, please?

SYBIL I'm just off to the kitchen, Basil.

BASIL   *(muttering angrily)* Yes, well, if you're too busy . . .

SYBIL   Nice to have met you, Lord Melbury. I hope
             you enjoy your stay. *(she leaves)*

MELBURY   Thank you so much.

BASIL   Yes, well I'll do it then, then I'll do the
             picture . . . *(suddenly polite again)* I'll put this away
             in one moment, your lord. *(to Manuel, who has
             appeared at last)* Manuel, will you take these
             cases to room twenty-one.

MANUEL   . . . *Qué?*

BASIL   Take . . . to room . . . twenty-one. *(he
             surreptitiously*[15] *signals the number with his fingers)*

MANUEL   . . . *No entender.*

BASIL   *Prenda las casos en* . . . oh, doesn't matter. Right!
             I'll do it, I'll do it. Thank you, Manuel. *(picks up
             the cases)*

MANUEL   I take them. *(grabs cases)*

BASIL   *(not letting go)* No, no, go away!

MANUEL   *Qué? (they struggle)*

BASIL   Go and wait!

MANUEL   Wait?

BASIL   *(indicating the dining room)* In there! Go and wait
             in there! Go and be a waiter in there! *(Manuel
             runs off; to Melbury)* I do apologize, your lord-
             ship. I'm afraid he's only just joined us.

---

[15]***surreptitiously***   secretively, not wanting to be seen

We're training him. It'd be quicker to train
a monkey, ha ha ha!

*Basil's laugh freezes as Melbury does not react. Then he
goes upstairs with the cases, reappearing a moment later.*

BASIL   Do please follow me . . . I mean, if you're
ready. There's no hurry . . .

MELBURY   Oh yes, yes, fine. *(follows Basil upstairs)*

*The dining room. Guests are eating peacefully until Basil
rushes in and goes to the window table where Mr and Mrs
Wareing and their son are eating.*

BASIL   Excuse me, I'm so sorry to bother you. Would
you mind moving to that table?

MR WAREING   . . . What?

BASIL   Could I ask you please to move to that table
over there?

MR WAREING   But . . .

BASIL   I'm so sorry to trouble you.

MR WAREING   *(getting up, protesting)* We're halfway through . . .

BASIL   Thank you so much.

MR WAREING   Yes, but . . .

BASIL   This is Lord Melbury's table, you see.

MR WAREING   What?

BASIL   Lord Melbury. When he stays with us he
always sits at this table.

MR WAREING   Well, why did they put us here?

BASIL Ah, an oversight . . . on my wife's part. I'm so sorry. He's just arrived, you see. Would you mind? – Polly! – Would you help these people to that table? Thank you, thank you so much.

The family get up very unwillingly. Polly, slightly puzzled, starts moving the dishes. Mrs Wareing is particularly slow. . .

BASIL Come on! **Come on!!** . . . Thank you. *(they move; Basil grabs a vase of flowers from another table and puts it on Melbury's; Melbury enters)* Ah, Lord Melbury! Do please come this way . . . your lordship . . . I have your table over here by the window . . . as usual . . . *(gives Melbury a slight wink, but gets no reaction)* Just here . . . thank you so much.

MELBURY Thank you, thank you very much . . .

Basil holds Melbury's chair, but moves it back just as Melbury sits down. Melbury falls, knocking the table over. Basil clouts Manuel, who happens to be passing.

BASIL I'm so sorry! Oh my Lord! Oh my God!!

MR WAREING *(to his wife)* I think he's killed him!

BASIL Get on with your meals!!! Thank you so much. *(he starts trying to make amends)*

In reception: Basil is at the desk doing the pools. Melbury comes out of the dining room wiping himself down with a handkerchief.

BASIL Lord Melbury, I really must apologize again for . . .

MELBURY Please, please, think nothing of it.

BASIL But it was so . . .

MELBURY Please! It was the smallest of accidents. It could have occurred anywhere.

BASIL Yes, but . . .

MELBURY No, no, no, I've forgotten all about it.

BASIL That's most . . . you're really . . . er, your lordship, would you allow me to offer you dinner here tonight . . . as our guest?

MELBURY That's extremely kind of you. Unfortunately I have an engagement tonight . . .

BASIL (mortified)[16] Oh!

MELBURY Oh actually . . .

BASIL Yes?

MELBURY There is one thing.

BASIL Good! Good!

MELBURY I was wondering . . . can you cash me a small cheque?[17] I'm playing golf this afternoon.

BASIL Oh, delighted!

MELBURY And I'd rather not go into the town . . .

BASIL Absolutely . . . I mean, er, how much? . . . er, if it's not a rude question.

MELBURY Er well . . . er . . . could you manage . . . fif . . . (looks in his wallet) Oh! . . . a hundred?

---

[16]**mortified** extremely upset
[17]**cash me a small cheque?** Melbury gives Basil a cheque and Basil gives him cash in return

BASIL   (*stunned*) A . . . h . . . hundred? (*recovering*) Oh
           absolutely . . . Oh yes, I mean, will a hundred
           be enough? . . . I mean a hundred and fifty . . .
           two . . . two . . . er, a hundred and sixty?

MELBURY . . . Let's see, that's, er, dinner tonight . . . few
           tips . . . oh, and it's the weekend, isn't it . . . is
           two hundred all right?

BASIL   (*momentarily shattered*) Oh! (*extravagantly*[18]) Oh!
           Please! Yes! Oh, ha, ha! – oh, tremendous!
           Oh . . . I'm so happy! I'll send someone to the
           town straightaway and have it for you here
           when you get back.

MELBURY Yes, well, that would be splendid.

BASIL   Thank you, thank you, your lordship.

MELBURY Thank you so much.

BASIL   Oh, not at all, my privilege . . . (*Melbury exits*) . . .
           What breeding . . . sheer . . . ooh! (*he starts to
           write the cheque, but Sybil walks in; he hides the book hur-
           riedly and gives her a peck on the cheek*) Hallo, dear.

SYBIL   What are you doing?

BASIL   I'm kissing you, dear.

SYBIL   Well, don't.

BASIL   Just thought it might be nice to . . .

SYBIL   I heard about lunch.

BASIL   What? . . . Oh, that! Oh, think nothing of it.

---

[18]***extravagantly***   with overdone generosity

SYBIL   What?

BASIL   It was the smallest of accidents. Could have
         occurred anywhere.

SYBIL   Anywhere? First you move that nice family in
         the middle of their meal, and then you attack
         Lord Melbury with a chair!

BASIL   Look, Sybil, I've had a word with Lord
         Melbury about it. He was quite charming . . .
         Oh, it's delightful to have people like that
         staying here . . . sheer class, golf, baths, engage-
         ments, a couple of hundr . . . h,h,horses . . .

SYBIL   Well, I've never seen such tatty cases.

BASIL   Of course you haven't. It's only the true upper
         class that would have tat like that . . . It's the

whole point! . . . Oh, you don't know what I'm talking about . . .

SYBIL   No I don't. But don't ever move guests in the middle of a meal again . . . and get that picture up. *(she goes into the office)*

BASIL   . . . Sour old rat. *(Polly comes in)* Ah! . . . Polly . . . would you do me a favour? When you're down in town this afternoon . . . just between ourselves, don't mention it to my wife . . . pop into the bank and just . . . *(writing the cheque . . .)*

In the town. Polly leaves the bank, crosses the street, and walks past a parked car. She checks, looks into it and is surprised to see Danny Brown sitting in it with another man. Danny sees her, motions her urgently to get into the car; she does so. He shows her an official-looking card and points to a jeweller's shop. At that moment Lord Melbury comes out of the shop, looks round furtively[19] and hurries down the street. Danny nods in the direction of a waiting colleague who follows Melbury. Danny and Polly watch . . .

Further reading

Scripts from all the episodes are published in *The Complete Fawlty Towers* (Methuen, 1998). Another television comedy series in which the characters find themselves in situations that are both funny and painful is *The Office* by Stephen Merchant and Ricky Gervais.

---

[19]***furtively***   secretively, as though up to something

Lord Arthur Savile's Crime

by Constance Cox, from a story by Oscar Wilde

Lord Arthur Savile has his palm read by a fortune-teller, and is told that he will one day commit a murder. Wanting to get the murder over and done with before his wedding day, he enlists the aid of his faithful manservant Baines. Between them they decide that the best plan will be to kill off one of Lord Arthur's elderly relatives. Accordingly Baines poisons one of the chocolates in a box to be given to Arthur's great-aunt, Lady Clementina. But just as they are about to send the box round to her house, there are some unexpected visitors: Sybil (Arthur's fiancée); Lady Julia (her mother); and Lady Windermere and the Dean (Arthur's aunt and uncle). Arthur has just been explaining to them all that Great-aunt Clementina is on the point of death when, most awkwardly, she turns up looking the picture of health!

LADY CLEMENTINA	Arthur dear, good morning. *(She kisses him)* Do you know, your stupid man tried to tell me you weren't in. Why, Lady Julia and dear Sybil. How nice to see you. Isn't it a perfectly beautiful morning? It feels wonderful to be alive.
LADY JULIA	In your condition, Lady Clementina, it would appear to be little short of miraculous.
LADY CLEMENTINA	*(moving c)*[1] My condition? Oh, has Arthur been telling you about my heartburn? You shouldn't take any notice of him. The dear boy exaggerates so.
LADY JULIA	*(grimly eyeing Arthur)* So it would seem.

[1]In the stage directions, *R*, *L* and *C* are 'right', 'left' and 'centre' of the stage *from the actors' point of view*; *up* means towards the back of the stage and *down* towards the front

LADY CLEMENTINA *(sitting in the armchair RC)* It has completely gone this morning, and so has my rheumatism. In fact when I woke up I felt so well I decided to give a little party tonight. I came to ask Arthur to arrange my music for me. He is so good at that sort of thing.

LADY JULIA *(looking at Arthur)* This is a most remarkable recovery.

ARTHUR *(nervously)* Yes – isn't it?

LADY CLEMENTINA Now go and find me some nice French music, Arthur. *(To Lady Julia)* I always have French songs at my parties; then people think they're hearing something they shouldn't, and it makes them so much happier. Go along, dear boy, and I shall sit here and have a nice gossip with Lady Julia and Sybil.

(ARTHUR moves reluctantly to the door up C)

LADY JULIA   We were on the point of leaving.

LADY   Oh, but you mustn't go.
CLEMENTINA

(LADY JULIA sits on the sofa. SYBIL sits on the chair down R)

I shall have no-one to talk to. *(She puts her gloves on the table RC and sees the box of sweets)* Oh, Arthur, is this a box of sweets? How nice!

ARTHUR   *(moving quickly above the table RC)* Oh, Auntie, please don't touch them.

LADY   *(seeing the card)* Why, they're for *me*. Oh,
CLEMENTINA   Arthur, how perfectly charming of you.

ARTHUR   I – I was going to send them round to you. I didn't want you to have them yet.

LADY   *(opening the box)* Then I'm very glad I came.
CLEMENTINA   I shall enjoy them all the sooner. *(She displays the box)* Don't they look delicious? And the dear boy never said a word about them.

SYBIL   Arthur is always so kind.

LADY   *(her hand hovering over the box)* Now, where
CLEMENTINA   shall I begin? Oh, how rude of me. I haven't offered them to you. *(She rises and crosses to the sofa)* Now, which will you have, Lady Julia? How about that nice pink one with the liquid centre?

(ARTHUR moves behind the sofa and holds his breath hopefully while LADY JULIA hesitates)

LADY JULIA	No – none of them, thank you.
LADY CLEMENTINA	Oh, won't you? *(She crosses to Sybil)* Well, Sybil, then?
SYBIL	*(rising and hesitating)* That pink one does look lovely. Are you sure you don't want it?
LADY CLEMENTINA	No, of course not. Do take it.

(SYBIL puts out her hand to take the capsule. ARTHUR plunges forward)

ARTHUR	No, Sybil, I forbid you. *(He snatches at her hand)* Here, have this one. *(He takes a sweet from the box and thrusts it into Sybil's mouth)*

(SYBIL nearly chokes. There are exclamations from the others. SYBIL collapses on to the chair down R, coughing)

LADY JULIA	Arthur, really!
LADY CLEMENTINA	Arthur, whatever are you thinking about?
ARTHUR	I'm sorry, Auntie, but if you knew the trouble I've been to – I mean, I chose them specially for you.
LADY CLEMENTINA	*(sitting in the armchair RC)* Now, isn't that nice of him? To choose sweets specially for me. Do you know, I believe Arthur is the only one of my relatives who'll be really sorry when I die.

(BAINES enters up C and stands R of the doorway)

BAINES	*(announcing)* Lady Windermere – the Dean of Paddington.
ARTHUR	Oh, Lord! *(He moves to the fireplace)*

(LADY WINDERMERE and the DEAN enter up C. The DEAN carries his umbrella. BAINES remains by the door)

LADY WINDERMERE	Good morning, Arthur. Your uncle was driving by so I said I'd come with him. Why, Clementina and Sybil, how nice. *(She glances briefly at Lady Julia, crosses and sits in the armchair down L)*
DEAN	*(crossing to Arthur and shaking hands)* You're not looking very well, my boy. Too much excitement at the moment, that's what it is. Well, Clementina – Lady Julia . . .
LADY CLEMENTINA	Robert, look at this beautiful box of sweets Arthur has just given me. You must each have one.
DEAN	*(moving to R of Lady Clementina)* Don't mind if I do. *(He takes a sweet)* *(LADY CLEMENTINA rises and crosses to Lady Windermere)*
LADY WINDERMERE	How nice. *(She takes a sweet)*
BAINES	*(to Arthur; questioningly)* My lord? *(ARTHUR moves to Baines and draws him aside up C)*
ARTHUR	Baines, she found them and I can't stop her. I don't even know if *it's* still there.
BAINES	One moment, my lord. *(He crosses to the Dean)* May I have your umbrella, your reverence?
DEAN	What? *(He realizes he still carries his umbrella)* Oh, I thought I'd left it in the hall. Thank you. *(BAINES takes the umbrella and returns to Arthur)*
BAINES	*It* is still there, my lord. *(He puts the umbrella L of the sideboard)* *(LADY CLEMENTINA, LADY JULIA and LADY WINDERMERE are talking together)*

ARTHUR	Thank heavens! Baines, get that box away from her. I don't care how, but get it away until she goes.
LADY CLEMENTINA	Arthur, do go and get my music, there's a good boy. I can't stay long.
ARTHUR	Yes, Auntie, I'm going. *(Imploringly²)* Oh, Baines!
BAINES	Leave it to me, my lord.
	(ARTHUR exits up R. BAINES goes to the sideboard and pours six glasses of sherry)
DEAN	What's this nonsense about Arthur postponing his marriage?
LADY CLEMENTINA	Arthur? *(She sits R of Lady Julia on the sofa)*
DEAN	*(sitting in the armchair RC)* Yes. Sent me a note about it. That's why I came round.
LADY JULIA	It appears he is expecting some tragic news.
DEAN	What? Not lost any money, has he?
LADY CLEMENTINA	Of course he hasn't. Arthur doesn't gamble. But why should he put it off? Is somebody ill?
LADY JULIA	I hate to appear morbid, Lady Clementina, but he seems to think *you* are.
LADY CLEMENTINA	I? What nonsense!
LADY JULIA	Unless, of course, this is some subterfuge³ for putting off the marriage altogether. I thought

²*Imploringly*   pleading
³**subterfuge**   false excuse, to hide the real motive

he had a furtive look when I came in – if Arthur's face can be said to convey any reasonable expression.

(BAINES picks up the tray of sherry and crosses to Sybil)

SYBIL
(taking a glass of sherry) You know that isn't true, Mamma. He was dreadfully anxious, and to be quite truthful, Lady Clementina, it *was* about you.

(BAINES crosses to LADY WINDERMERE, who takes a glass of sherry)

LADY CLEMENTINA
I suppose it was because I told him I felt a little unwell yesterday. But I shall be fit as a fiddle for your wedding, my dear, and you must tell him not to dream of a postponement.

(BAINES moves to LADY JULIA, who takes a glass of sherry)

Now, who is going to have another of my delicious sweets?

LADY WINDERMERE
Not just now, Clem, thank you.

LADY CLEMENTINA
Then Robert? *(She rises and moves to the Dean)* Do try that exciting looking pink one with the liquid centre.

DEAN
(about to take the capsule) Oh, thank you.
(BAINES moves quickly to the Dean)

BAINES
Sherry, your reverence?

DEAN
What? Oh, after my sherry, Clementina. *(He takes a glass of sherry)*

BAINES   *(offering the tray to Lady Clementina)* My lady?

LADY CLEMENTINA   *(moving and sitting R of Lady Julia on the sofa)* No, no sherry for me. I am forbidden it. There is really no pleasure in being an invalid now-adays. They have so many disagreeable devices for getting one well again. *(She places the box on the right arm of the sofa)*

BAINES   *(moving to R of the sofa)* May I recommend a little port, your ladyship? His lordship keeps a very superior brand. *(He rests the tray on the box)*

LADY CLEMENTINA   *(doubtfully)* Well . . .

LADY WINDERMERE   Just this once, Clementina, to drink Arthur's health in.

LADY CLEMENTINA   Well, just this once. A very little, Baines.

BAINES   Yes, my lady. *(He manages to pick up the box with his tray and goes to the sideboard. During the next speech, he pours a glass of port, with his back to the others)*

LADY CLEMENTINA   And now that I have the opportunity, I want to invite you all to my little party tonight. I hope none of you will refuse an old woman whose last pleasure this may be.

(There are general murmurs of 'delighted', 'a great pleasure', etc. BAINES, unseen by the others, takes the capsule from the box of sweets, and holds it poised over the glass of port)

Good. That's settled. Baines, you are giving me only a very little? I mustn't have anything that will make me ill.

BAINES	*(dropping the capsule in the glass)* I assure you you will feel nothing, my lady. *(He gently revolves the glass and takes it to Lady Clementina)*
LADY CLEMENTINA	*(taking the glass)* Thank you. Now, see if my carriage has returned. I sent my maid in it to do a little shopping.
BAINES	Very good, my lady. *(He moves to the doors up C)* *(ARTHUR enters up R, carrying some music)*
ARTHUR	Everybody being looked after, Baines?
BAINES	*(significantly)* All is well, my lord.
ARTHUR	*(excitedly)* You mean . . .? *(BAINES opens his mouth and points to it, then points to Lady Clementina and nods)*
ARTHUR	*(fervently)* Thank you, Baines. *(He puts the music on the table behind the sofa)* *(BAINES exits up C. ARTHUR, in high spirits, moves down C)*
LADY WINDERMERE	Ah, Arthur, you're just in time. We were about to drink your health and Sybil's.
ARTHUR	Thank you, Auntie.
LADY CLEMENTINA	I am indulging in[4] some of your excellent port, Arthur, although it is really poison to me. But I would suffer anything for you, dear boy.
ARTHUR	Oh, you won't suffer anything now, Auntie. Do you feel all right? *(He sits on the right arm of the sofa)*

---

[4]**indulging in**   allowing myself to have

LADY CLEMENTINA	Perfectly well, darling. *(She raises her glass)* Now – to Sybil and Arthur.
DEAN LADY WINDERMERE LADY JULIA	*(together)* To Sybil and Arthur.

(They are about to drink when SYBIL speaks)

SYBIL	*(rising)* Lady Clem, I know it's dreadful of me, but . . .
LADY CLEMENTINA	*(lowering her glass)* What is it, dear?
SYBIL	I would love you to drink our healths – really I would – but please don't if it means it would make you ill.
ARTHUR	Oh, I don't think it would make any difference now, Sybil. *(To Lady Clementina)* Are you still feeling all right, Auntie?
LADY CLEMENTINA	A little tired, that's all. It's the excitement.
ARTHUR	Yes, of course. I should go home and lie down quietly on your bed if I were you. I'll send round in a couple of hours to see how you are.
LADY CLEMENTINA	Dear boy, he is always so solicitous for[5] me. *(To Sybil)* Very well, child, I won't drink this if it will make you unhappy. Arthur shall have it instead. It will do him good.

(SYBIL resumes her seat)

---

[5]**solicitous for**   concerned and considerate about

ARTHUR	Are you sure you don't want it, Auntie?
LADY CLEMENTINA	*(handing the glass to Arthur)* No, no, you have it. *(To the others)* He looked so pale when I came in, but now he's looking much better.
DEAN	And you'll feel a lot different, my boy, with that inside you. *(He rises)* Now – to Sybil and Arthur. *(He drinks)*
	(LADY JULIA and LADY WINDERMERE rise and drink)
SYBIL	*(rising and raising her glass)* To you, Arthur.
ARTHUR	*(rising and raising his glass)* To you, Sybil darling, and all the years ahead of us.
	(SYBIL and ARTHUR drink. ARTHUR drains the glass of port to the dregs then puts the glass on the table RC)
LADY JULIA	*(putting her glass on the table behind the sofa)* Now, Sybil, it is time we were leaving. You are due at your milliner's.[6] I take it, Arthur, there need be no more talk about postponing the wedding? *(She moves up LC)*
ARTHUR	*(moving up C)* Oh, no, Lady Julia. Now I know how I stand with Lady Clem we can carry on with our original arrangements.
	(SYBIL moves up RC. The DEAN takes Sybil's glass and puts it with his own on the mantelpiece)
LADY JULIA	I am very glad to hear it.
	(BAINES enters up C and stands R of the doorway. LADY WINDERMERE puts her glass on the table behind the sofa. LADY CLEMENTINA rises and picks up the music from the table behind the sofa)

---

[6]milliner's hat-maker's

Are you coming, Lady Windermere?

DEAN *(moving C)* I'm going along now, Margaret. I can give you a lift. *(To Arthur)* Good-bye, my boy.
(He moves up C and collects his umbrella)
(ARTHUR is kissing Sybil)

LADY JULIA Good morning, Arthur. *Sybil*!
(The DEAN, LADY WINDERMERE, LADY JULIA and SYBIL exit up C. LADY CLEMENTINA moves up C)

BAINES *(to Lady Clementina)* Your carriage has returned, my lady.

LADY CLEMENTINA Thank you, Baines. Now, where are my lovely sweets? Oh, they're on that sideboard. Get them for me, Arthur. I can't think how they came to be over there.
(ARTHUR collects the box of sweets and hands them to Lady Clementina)
I've nearly eaten them all. Wasn't that greedy of me? But they were so delicious.

ARTHUR I'm so glad you enjoyed them. Go home and lie down quietly now.
(LADY CLEMENTINA kisses Arthur)

LADY CLEMENTINA I shall see you tonight, dear boy, and afterwards in church.

ARTHUR That's right, Auntie.
(LADY CLEMENTINA exits up C.
BAINES follows her off. ARTHUR exhales triumphantly and moves down RC, humming 'The Wedding March'. BAINES enters up C)

So you did it, Baines. I'm extremely grateful to
you. When I went out I was paralysed with
fright that something would happen to Miss
Merton. How did you get Lady Clem to take
the right one?

BAINES   *(moving down c)* It was quite simple, my lord.
I foresaw the danger the indiscriminate[7]
handing round of the sweets might lead
to, so on serving the sherry I took the
opportunity of surreptitiously[8] removing
the box.

ARTHUR   *(crossing below the sofa)* Ah, yes, and then?

BAINES   Lady Clementina requested a glass of port,
my lord. I was just pouring it out when I
suddenly remembered that the capsule
dissolved readily[9] in liquid. I took the
fatal potion from the box and dropped
it in the port.

ARTHUR   The glass of port – you gave to – Lady Clem?

BAINES   Yes, my lord.

ARTHUR   You – put the poison in it?

BAINES   I did, my lord, and as you see, her ladyship
drained it to the dregs. *(He picks up the glass
from the table RC and displays it)* We should
expect the happy news in about half an
hour, my lord.

---

[7]**indiscriminate**   random and uncontrolled
[8]**surreptitiously**   secretively, not wanting to be seen
[9]**readily**   easily

ARTHUR   *(collapsing on to the sofa)* You blithering idiot! You infernal nincompoop!

BAINES   My lord!

ARTHUR   *I* drank it!

Further reading

Constance Cox's play is loosely based on a short story of the same name by Oscar Wilde. If you read it you will see that it has a more serious tone than this spin-off. The funniest novels featuring a clever servant and dim master (like Baines and Lord Arthur) are the Jeeves and Wooster books by P. G. Wodehouse.

The Alchemist

by Ben Jonson

A clever servant called Face takes advantage of the fact that his master has left London to avoid the plague. He invites two accomplices into the house: a crook called Subtle and a prostitute, Dol Common. Together they devise a plan to cheat people out of their money, in which Subtle pretends to be an alchemist – a mixture of scientist and magician. A number of clients quickly turn up at their door, all hoping to make money in one way or another. One of these is a fashionable young lawyer, Dapper, who hopes that 'the alchemist' will be able to furnish him with a 'familiar' spirit which will enable him to win at dice.

Instantly spotting Dapper for a sucker, Subtle and Face tell him that he is incredibly fortunate: the Queen of the Fairies is no less a person than Dapper's own aunt! To meet her, they say, he must first perform certain magic ceremonies: put on a clean shirt, stick vinegar up his nose, and cry 'hum' and 'buz' three times.

Excited by the belief that he will soon meet his aunt the Queen of the Fairies, Dapper returns later.

FACE	Come on, master Dapper,
	You see how I turn clients here away,
	To give your cause dispatch;[1] have you perform'd
	The ceremonies were enjoin'd you?[2]
DAPPER	Yes, of the vinegar,
	And the clean shirt.
FACE	'Tis well: that shirt may do you
	More worship[3] than you think. Your aunt's a-fire,

[1]**give your cause dispatch** speed up your business
[2]**were enjoin'd you** you were told to do
[3]**worship** good

But that she will not shew it, t' have a sight of
you.
Have you provided for her grace's servants?

DAPPER   Yes, here are six score[4] Edward shillings.[5]

FACE   Good!

DAPPER   And an old Harry's sovereign.

FACE   Very good!

DAPPER   And three James shillings, and an Elizabeth
groat, Just twenty nobles.

FACE   O, you are too just.
I would you had had the other noble in Maries.

DAPPER   I have some Philip and Maries.

FACE   Ay, those same

Are best of all: where are they? *(There is a knock
at the door)* Hark, the doctor.

*SUBTLE enters, dressed like a fairy 'priest', carrying a rag
of torn cloth.*

SUBTLE   *(disguising his voice)* Is yet her grace's cousin
come?

FACE   He is come.

SUBTLE   And is he fasting?[6]

FACE   Yes.

---

[4]**six score**   one hundred and twenty
[5]**Edward shillings ... Harry's sovereign ... James shillings ... Elizabeth
groat ... nobles ... Philip and Maries**   all coins, some named after
kings and queens; 'twenty nobles' is about thirty-three pounds
[6]**fasting**   going without food

SUBTLE   And hath cried 'Hum'?

FACE   *(To Dapper)* 'Thrice',[7] you must answer.

DAPPER   Thrice.

SUBTLE   And as oft 'Buz'?

FACE   *(To Dapper)* If you have, say.

DAPPER   I have.

SUBTLE   Then, to her cuz,[8]
(Speaking in 'fairy' verse)

Hoping that he hath vinegar'd his senses,
As he was bid, the Fairy queen dispenses,
By me, this robe, the petticoat of fortune;
Which that he straight put on, she doth
       importune.[9]
He hands DAPPER a dirty old skirt, which he puts on.

And though to fortune near be her petticoat,
Yet nearer is her smock,[10] the queen doth note:
And therefore, ev'n of that a piece she hath sent
Which, being[11] a child, to wrap him in was
       rent;[12]
And prays him for a scarf he now will wear it,
With as much love as then her grace did tear it,
About his eyes, to shew he is fortunate.
They tie a rag from an old smock round his eyes.

---

[7]**Thrice**   three times
[8]**cuz**   cousin or any family relative (they have told him he is the Fairy
    Queen's nephew)
[9]**importune**   beg
[10]**smock**   a garment like a nightgown worn under the dress
[11]**being**   when he was
[12]**rent**   torn

> And, trusting unto her to make his state,[13]
> He'll throw away all worldly pelf[14] about him;
> Which that he will perform, she doth not
>   doubt him.

FACE   *(Aside to Subtle)* She need not doubt him, sir.
>   Alas, he has nothing,
> But what he will part withal[15] as willingly,
> Upon her grace's word! *(To Dapper)* Throw
>   away your purse
> As she would ask it – handkerchiefs and all –

Dapper throws his purse away.

> *(Aside to Subtle)* She cannot bid that thing, but
>   he'll obey.[16]
> *(To Dapper)* If you have a ring about you, cast it
>   off,
> Or a silver seal at your wrist; her grace will send
> Her fairies here to search you, therefore deal
> Directly[17] with her highness: if they find
> That you conceal a mite,[18] you are undone.[19]

DAPPER   Truly, there's all.

FACE   All what?

DAPPER   My money; truly.

---

[13]**make his state**   make him a wealthy man
[14]**pelf**   riches
[15]**withal**   with
[16]**She cannot bid . . .**   there's nothing she can ask that he won't do
[17]**Directly**   honestly, frankly
[18]**a mite**   the tiniest coin
[19]**undone**   finished, ruined

FACE   Keep nothing that is transitory[20] about you.

(Aside to SUBTLE) Bid Dol play music.
Dol plays the cittern[21] in another room.

Look, the elves are come

To pinch you, if you tell not truth! Advise you!
SUBTLE and FACE pinch him.

DAPPER   O! I have a paper with a Spur Ryal[22] in't.

FACE   *(Imitating a 'fairy' sound) Ti, ti!*

They knew't, they say.

SUBTLE   *(Copying Face's sound) Ti, ti, ti, ti.* He has more yet.

FACE   *Ti, ti-ti-ti. (Aside to SUBTLE)* In the other pocket.

SUBTLE   *Titi, titi, titi, titi, titi.*

They must pinch him or he will never confess,
they say.

They pinch him again. DAPPER cries out.

*In the following exchanges, FACE keeps switching from his
fairy voice to his own.*

FACE   *(As though addressing the 'fairies')* Nay, pray you,
hold:[23] he is her grace's nephew,

(In his fairy voice) Ti, ti, ti?

(As though to the fairies again) What care you?
Good faith, you shall care.

---

[20]**transitory**   not everlasting: in other words, worldly possessions
[21]*cittern*   instrument like a lute or guitar
[22]**Spur Ryal**   another coin
[23]**hold**   stop

> (*To DAPPER*) Deal plainly, sir, and shame the
> fairies. Shew
>
> You are innocent.

DAPPER   By this good light, I have nothing.

SUBTLE   *Ti, ti, ti, ti, to, ta.* He does equivocate[24] she says:
> *Ti, ti do ti, ti ti do, ti da;*
> and swears by the light when he is blinded.

DAPPER   By this good dark, I have nothing but a
> half-crown[25]
> Of gold about my wrist, that my love gave me;
> And a leaden heart I wore since she forsook[26]
> me.

FACE   I thought 'twas something. And would you
> incur
> Your aunt's displeasure[27] for these trifles?[28]
> Come,
> I had rather you had thrown away twenty
> half-crowns.
>
> *Dapper reluctantly takes the half-crown off his wrist.*
>
> You may wear your leaden heart still.

Suddenly Dol rushes in to tell them that another of their 'cus-
tomers', Sir Epicure Mammon, has arrived. Not wanting to lose
Dapper, they thrust him into a stinking lavatory, blindfolded and
with a gag of gingerbread in his mouth – a gift, they say, from his
aunt, the queen of the fairies.

---

[24]**He does equivocate**   he is not telling the whole truth
[25]**half-crown**   a coin, one-eighth of a pound
[26]**forsook**   left, deserted
[27]**incur . . . Your aunt's displeasure**   make your aunt angry with you
[28]**trifles**   insignificant bits and pieces

> Hours later, having been frantically busy with other customers, FACE and SUBTLE suddenly remember that DAPPER has been left in the lavatory all the while . . .

SUBTLE enters, bringing in DAPPER, his eyes still bound.

SUBTLE   How! you have eaten your gag?

DAPPER   Yes faith, it crumbled
Away in my mouth.

SUBTLE   You have spoil'd all then.

DAPPER   No!
I hope my aunt of Fairy will forgive me.

SUBTLE   Your aunt's a gracious lady; but in troth
You were to blame.

DAPPER   The fume[29] did overcome me,
And I did do't to stay my stomach.[30] 'Pray you
So satisfy[31] her grace.

FACE   *(Aside to SUBTLE)* Show him his aunt, and let
him be dispatch'd:[32]
I'll send her to you.
FACE exits.

SUBTLE   Well, sir, your aunt her grace
Will give you audience presently,[33] on my suit,[34]
And the captain's word that you did not eat
your gag

---

[29]**fume**   smell
[30]**stay my stomach**   stop myself being hungry
[31]**pray you, so satisfy**   I beg you, explain to
[32]**dispatch'd**   sent on his way
[33]**presently**   straight away
[34]**on my suit**   at my request

In any contempt[35] of her highness.

SUBTLE unbinds DAPPER's eyes.

DAPPER   Not I, in troth, sir.

DOL enters, dressed like the Queen of the Fairies.

SUBTLE   Here she is come. Down o' your knees and
            wriggle:
        She has a stately presence.

DAPPER kneels and shuffles towards her.

        Good! Yet nearer,
        And bid, God save you!

DAPPER   Madam!

SUBTLE   And your aunt.

DAPPER   And my most gracious aunt, God save your
            grace.

DOL   *(In a 'fairy' voice)* Nephew, we thought to have
            been angry with you;
        But that sweet face of yours hath turn'd the tide,
        And made it flow with joy, that ebb'd of love.[36]
        Arise, and touch our velvet gown.

SUBTLE   The skirts,
        And kiss 'em. So!

DAPPER kisses DOL's skirt.

DOL   Let me now stroke that head.
        (She chants) 'Much, nephew, shalt thou win,
            much shalt thou spend,

---

[35]**contempt**   lack of respect
[36]**ebb'd of love**   because he had eaten the gingerbread, her love for him had
lessened, like the tide going out

Much shalt thou give away, much shalt thou
    lend.'

SUBTLE   *(aside)* Ay, much! indeed.
          (To DAPPER) Why do you not thank her grace?

DAPPER   I cannot speak for joy.

SUBTLE   See, the kind wretch!
          Your grace's kinsman right.

DOL   Give me the bird.

*SUBTLE hands Dol a dead bird in a purse, which she hangs
around DAPPER's neck – this is the 'familiar spirit' that
DAPPER wanted to help him win when gambling.*

Here is your fly[37] in a purse, about your neck,
    cousin;
Wear it, and feed it about this day sev'n-night,[38]
On your right wrist.

SUBTLE   Open a vein with a pin,
          And let it suck but once a week; till then,
          You must not look on't.

DOL   No: and kinsman,
          Bear yourself worthy of the blood you come on.[39]

DAPPER   By this hand, I will.

SUBTLE   You may bring's[40] a thousand pound
          Before to-morrow night, if but three
              thousand
          Be stirring, an you will.

---

[37]**fly**   familiar spirit
[38]**this day sev'n-night**   a week's time
[39]**on**   from
[40]**bring's**   bring us

DAPPER   I swear I will then.

SUBTLE   Your fly will learn[41] you all games.

FACE   *(Calling from another room)* Have you done there?

SUBTLE   Your grace will command him no more duties?

DOL   No:
But come, and see me often. I may chance
To leave him three or four hundred chests of
        treasure,
And some twelve thousand acres of fairy land,
If he game well and comely[42] with good
        gamesters.[43]

SUBTLE   There's a kind aunt! Kiss her departing part.[44]
But you must sell your forty mark a year,[45] now.

DAPPER   Ay, sir, I mean.[46]

SUBTLE   Or, give't away; pox on't!

DAPPER   I'll give't mine aunt. I'll go and fetch the
writings.[47]

    He leaves.

---

[41]**learn**   teach
[42]**game well and comely**   gambles successfully and with the right people
[43]**gamesters**   gamblers
[44]**her departing part**   her behind
[45]**forty mark a year**   Dapper's annual income
[46]**mean**   mean to
[47]**writings**   legal documents (so that he can sign over his money to his 'aunt')

Further reading

Another Ben Jonson play featuring notorious crooks trying to cheat rich and foolish people out of their money is *Volpone*. One famous story about an alchemist, even older than Ben Jonson's, is *The Canon's Yeoman's Tale*, one of the *Canterbury Tales* by Geoffrey Chaucer.

Activities

Wyrd Sisters

Before you read

1   In groups, talk about the presentation of witches in books and films. You might know Shakespeare's *Macbeth*, J.K. Rowling's Harry Potter series, Philip Pullman's *Northern Lights* (made into the film *The Golden Compass*), or C.S. Lewis's *The Lion, the Witch and the Wardrobe*.

What's it about?

2   A great deal of the comedy in this play derives from the fact that people do not behave as we expect them to. For example, the Duke is supposed to be a ruthless killer, but is instead a cowardly bungler. In what ways are the witches and their way of life not what we expect? Think about:
   ● their day-to-day language and the familiar way in which they address each other
   ● the objects they use to cast their spell
   ● the attitude and behaviour of the Demon
   ● the witches' treatment of the Demon.

3   When Scene 8 opens, how would an audience know that they were in a typical medieval castle's torture-chamber? Think about the sound effects in the opening stage directions and the objects on stage.

Thinking about the text

4   Stephen Briggs's stage directions are an important part of the script. Find examples of stage directions which:
   ● tell actors when to enter
   ● tell them which physical actions they should perform
   ● tell them how to react
   ● tell them when to pause
   ● offer suggestions about how to make special effects work on stage
   ● describe what we see when a new scene opens
   ● tell us which lighting and sound effects the audience will see and hear.

Fawlty Towers: A Touch of Class

Before you read

1   In a modern play, how would you dress a teacher, doctor, gardener
so that the audience can immediately recognize what job they do?

What's it about?

2   *Fawlty Towers* is famous as one of the great television situation
comedy series. In groups, find examples of the different kinds of
comedy in this extract. One example of each kind has been given to
start you off:
- visual comedy (the grapefruit)
- verbal comedy (the misprints on the menu)
- comedy of character (Basil's reaction to Melbury)
- situation comedy (Basil's various uncompleted jobs).

Which is your favourite kind of comedy in this extract?

Thinking about the text

3   In pairs, look back at the dialogue between Basil and Danny
Brown. Brown is described in the stage directions as '*a very non-
aristocratic-looking cockney*'. What do you notice about the way
Danny Brown speaks? Re-read the dialogue and think of an appropriate accent for Danny Brown.

Now find an accent for Lord Melbury. Again, how would you
describe it?

Discuss why Brown and Melbury have such different ways of
speaking.

4   Re-read the final stage directions ('*In the town . . . Polly watch . . .*').

Who is Danny Brown? Who are the other men? Why are they
watching Melbury? What is Melbury up to?

Write a paragraph describing how you think the story about Basil
and Lord Melbury might end.

Lord Arthur Savile's Crime

Before you read

1   In groups, talk about stories you know in which someone plans to commit a murder. You might recall tales from childhood, such as *Snow White*; stories such as Edgar Allan Poe's *The Tell-Tale Heart*; or plays such as *Macbeth* and *Richard III*. What kind of plans do the plotters have to make to avoid detection? What often goes wrong?

What's it about?

2   *Lord Arthur Savile's Crime* is a play that involves a great deal of physical comedy. In groups of four, rehearse the episode in which the chocolates are being handed round. You will need a 'prop' box of chocolates. Try to get across the women's innocence and Arthur's growing panic.

3   In real life murder is not funny; and yet on stage or screen it has often been the subject of comedy. As a class, discuss how the play manages to:
   a   create suspense, as in a serious murder story
   b   at the same time make us laugh.

Thinking about the text

4   Arthur is an extremely funny character. He isn't very bright, and, as circumstances change, his mood keeps shifting from cheerfulness to despair and back again. Re-read the extract. How would you describe Arthur's mood at the following moments:
   • when he is told by Lady Clementina to go and find some music
   • when Lady Clementina first spots the chocolates
   • when Sybil reaches out to select the poisoned chocolate
   • when Baines announces the arrival of Lady Windermere and the Dean of Paddington
   • when Baines assures him that everything is all right?
   • when Baines is halfway through explaining how he poisoned Lady Clementina's drink
   • at the very end of the scene?

The Alchemist

Before you read

1   In Jonson's time many people believed in the powers of alchemy, and as a result were cheated by con-men claiming that they had special powers. As a class, share stories of people being cheated by clever and unscrupulous crooks. You might have heard about 'scams' in the news, for example, or have read a book or seen a film in which this kind of thing happens.

What's it about?

2   In groups of three, act out the beginning of the extract, where Face and Subtle persuade Dapper to wear a dirty skirt and a blindfold and give up all his money and possessions.

- Face and Subtle: Enjoy yourselves! Create a funny 'Ti, ti, ti' sound for the fake fairies. Try to vary the sound to convey different meanings.
- Dapper: Act a mixture of fear and excitement – but never forget that you are greedy for the special powers that your 'aunt' will give you.

The scene will be more fun if you use costume: you will need an old skirt and a length of rag.

3   Imagine that one of Dapper's friends asks him later about his visit to the alchemist's. Unaware of how stupid he has been, he tells his friend exactly what happened. In pairs, role-play the conversation. Think about:

- why Dapper went to the house in the first place
- what happened on each of his visits
- how he was left feeling at the end
- what he is now required to do.

Thinking about the text

4   Imagine you are planning a performance of The Alchemist. In pairs, design the costumes that Subtle wears as the Fairy Priest, and that Dol wears as Queen of the Fairies. Remember that they are likely to be using things they have found about the house. Decide first whether you are setting the play in Ben Jonson's own time (it was first performed in 1610), or today.

Compare and contrast

1   This final section is devoted to plays that are designed to make us laugh. In small groups discuss which one you thought was funniest and explain what particularly amused and entertained you.

2   Look back at the four extracts and, in small groups, find examples of:
   - verbal comedy (where we laugh at what people say)
   - physical comedy (where we laugh at what they do)
   - situation comedy (where we laugh at the situation they are in).

   Pick a short scene that has good examples of all three types of comedy and rehearse it to bring out as much of the humour as you can. Then perform it for the class.

3   *The Alchemist* was written in the early 17th century; *Lord Arthur Savile's Crime* is a modern play written in the language of the 19th century; while *Fawlty Towers* and *Wyrd Sisters* are both 20th-century plays.

   Use examples from these four plays to write a short essay entitled 'Comedy through the Ages', showing how some aspects of humour have changed and some have remained the same.

4   Write a short extract from a new play in which characters from the four extracts in this section meet each other. Decide on a setting and work out a comic situation.

   For example, you could set your scene in the Fawlty Towers hotel and show what happens when Basil realises that his guests include Subtle (from *The Alchemist*), Granny (from *Wyrd Sisters*) and Lord Arthur Savile. How differently does he behave with each one? What tricky situation arises?

Notes on authors

Alan Bennett first became known as part of the *Beyond the Fringe* satirical review in the early 1960s, but since then he has become one of Britain's best known playwrights, screen-writers and autobiographers. Much of his writing draws upon his early years growing up in Leeds, Yorkshire.

Eric Bergren is an American writer who co-wrote the screenplay of *The Elephant Man* with David Lynch and Christopher De Vore.

Stephen Briggs loves to be involved in the amateur drama of Abingdon, Oxfordshire, where he adapted Terry Pratchett's novel *Wyrd Sisters* for the stage and also played the original Duke Felmet. You can learn about his *Discworld* adaptations on his website http://www.stephenbriggs.com

Connie Booth is an American actress who appeared in a number of British television comedies and co-wrote the hugely successful *Fawlty Towers* with her husband at the time **John Cleese**. She now works as a psychotherapist in London and is involved in a project helping single mothers.

David Calcutt lives in Walsall, West Midlands, where he works as a playwright and storyteller, greatly influenced by mythology and folktales. Having been a teacher for ten years, much of his writing has been for younger audiences, but he has also had a number of plays performed on BBC radio.

John Cleese became famous as part of the *Monty Python* team, but for most people his greatest achievement is *Fawlty Towers* which he co-wrote and performed with his wife **Connie Booth**. The series came top of the British Film Institute's list of the hundred best British television programmes (*Blackadder* was second).

Paul Cornell is a novelist and playwright best known for his writing for television where he has produced scripts for *Robin Hood*, *Casualty* and *Coronation Street*. He also writes for several British comics and for Marvel comics in the USA. You can read more about him on his blog: http://paulcornell.blogspot.com

Constance Cox (1912–1998) was a script-writer who specialised in adapting nineteenth century novels for stage and television. She won a major award for her script of *The Forsyte Saga*, a great hit on BBC television in 1967.

Richard Curtis was born in New Zealand but came to England when he was eleven. He met Rowan Atkinson at Oxford University and the friendship led to their working together in *Blackadder* (which he co-wrote mainly with **Ben Elton**) and *Mr Bean*. Since then he has written a number of highly successful scripts for the screen, including *Four Weddings and a Funeral* and *The Vicar of Dibley*.

Christopher De Vore is an American screenwriter. In addition to co-writing *The Elephant Man* with David Lynch and Eric Bergren, he worked on the film adaptation of William Shakespeare's *Hamlet*, which starred Mel Gibson.

David Edgar became famous for his adaptation of Charles Dickens' *Nicholas Nickleby* (1980) which was named Best Play in London and won a Tony Award in the USA. Most of his plays since have contained political themes.

Ben Elton left university to become a successful stand-up comedian but soon became co-writer of the television sitcom *The Young Ones*. In 1985 he teamed up with **Richard Curtis** to write the second season of *Blackadder*, and they stayed together to produce *Blackadder the Third* and *Blackadder Goes Forth*. He is also a very popular novelist.

Susan Glaspell (1882–1948) was born in Iowa in the United States and began her working life as a journalist on local newspapers. One day she decided to turn her report of a murder trial into a play called *Trifles*. She wrote many best-selling novels and won the prestigious Pulitzer Prize, the highest honour an American writer can receive.

Lorraine Hansberry (1930–1965) was an African-American writer who was born in Chicago, USA. *A Raisin in the Sun* was first staged in 1959, and was immediately hailed as "The play that changed American theatre forever . . .". Not only was it by an African-American woman, it was a view of life among black Americans that nobody had represented on stage before. She died of cancer at only 34.

Ben Jonson (1572–1637) first worked as a bricklayer and then joined the army before becoming an actor and playwright. Having narrowly escaped execution for killing a fellow actor in a duel, Jonson became one of the most successful playwrights of his time with biting comedies such as *Volpone* and *The Alchemist*. William Shakespeare performed in some of his plays and the two became close friends.

David Lynch is an American film director, born in Montana in 1946. Living in a violent, run-down American city inspired his first major film, *Eraserhead*, in 1971. Since then his films have become known for their nightmarish quality. He co-wrote *The Elephant Man* with Christopher De Vore and Eric Bergren and has been nominated for an Academy Award (the Oscar) three times.

John O'Connor was born in London but now lives in Maryland, USA. His plays for young audiences include three under the overall title *Crimes and Punishments*, of which *Lad Carl* is one. Most of his time, however, he writes about Shakespeare and has published a trilogy of plays about Shakespeare's acting company.

George Bernard Shaw (1856–1950) is one of the most famous playwrights in the English language, the only one to have won both a Nobel Prize and an Academy Award (the Oscar). Shaw was an Irishman, but he spent nearly all his working life as a playwright in England. He wrote over sixty plays, mainly about social themes such as marriage, religion and class.

William Shakespeare (1564–1616) is the world's best known and most widely performed playwright. He wrote around forty plays, often divided into Comedies, Histories and Tragedies. His plays have lasted for four centuries, not least because people in every culture and every era have been able to discover their own new meanings in them and continue to do so.

Larry Shue (1946–1985) was an American playwright and actor, born in New Orleans. He is famous for two comedies from the early 1980s, *The Foreigner* and *The Nerd*, both still widely performed. His comedy is often based on mistaken identity or the confusions that arise when someone starts playing a role. He died in a plane crash when he was only 39.

Wole Soyinka was born in Nigeria in 1934. After a university education in Britain and a spell at the Royal Court Theatre London, he returned home to study African theatre. He was arrested in 1967 during the Nigerian civil war, but was released from prison two years later and has written over twenty plays, novels and poetry collections.

Oscar Wilde (1854–1900) was born in Ireland but became the most celebrated playwright in nineteenth-century London. His best known work, *The Importance of Being Earnest*, remains one of the most popular plays in the English language. Wilde is famed for his wit and was also a successful poet, critic and writer of fiction.

Acknowledgements

The volume editor and publishers acknowledge the following sources of copyright material and are grateful for the permissions granted. While every effort has been made, it has not always been possible to identify the sources of all the material used, or to trace all copyright holders. If any omissions are brought to our notice we will be happy to include the appropriate acknowledgements on reprinting.

p. 2: script extract from Doctor Who: Human Nature, written by Paul Cornell. Reproduced by permission of the author and the BBC; p. 15: 'The Elephant Man' screenplay by Christopher De Vore, Eric Bergen & David Lynch; p. 27: 'A Raisin in the Sun' by Lorraine Hansberry, published by Methuen Drama, an imprint of A&C Black, copyright © 1958 by Robert Nemiroff, as an unpublished work. Copyright © 1959, 1966, 1984 by Robert Nemiroff. Copyright renewed 1986, 1987 by Robert Nemiroff. Used by permission of Random House, Inc.; p. 37: 'Death and the King's Horseman' by Wole Soyinka, Copyright © 1975, 2003 by Wole Soyinka. Reprinted with permission by Melanie Jackson Agency, LLC; p. 62: 'The Life and Adventures of Nicholas Nickleby' by Charles Dickens, adapted for stage by David Edgar published by Methuen Drama, an imprint of A&C Black; p. 86: 'Treasure Island' by R. L. Stevenson, dramatised by David Calcutt. Reproduced with the permission of Nelson Thornes Ltd. from Dramascripts: Treasure Island, ISBN 978-0-17-432560-4, first published in 1999; p. 106: 'Trifles' by Susan Glaspell, used with permission of the Estate of Susan Glaspell; p. 119: 'Saint Joan' by George Bernard Shaw, by permission of The Society of Authors, on behalf of the Bernard Shaw Estate; p. 132: 'King Henry V' by William Shakespeare, edited by Marilyn Bell, Elizabeth Dane, John Dane, Cambridge School Shakespeare Series, 1993 © Cambridge University Press, reproduced with permission. p. 150: 'Lad Carl' a folktale dramatised by John O'Connor. Reproduced with the permission of Nelson Thornes Ltd. from Dramascripts: Crimes and Punishments, ISBN 978-0-17-432617-5, first published in 2000; p. 164: Extract from The Wind in the Willows adapted by Alan Bennett (© Forelake Ltd. 1991) from The Wind in the Willows by Kenneth Grahame is reproduced by permission of PFD (www.pfd.co.uk) on behalf of Forelake Ltd.; p. 184: 'Potato', words from Blackadder: The Whole Damn Dynasty (Michael Joseph, 1998) Copyright © Richard Curtis and Ben Elton,

1985; p. 190: 'The Foreigner' by Larry Shue, Copyright © 1985 by Larry Shue, 1983 by Larry Shue as an unpublished dramatic composition. Reprinted by permission of William Morris Agency on behalf of the Author's estate; p. 217: From 'Wyrd Sisters' by Terry Pratchett, adapted for stage by Stephen Briggs, published by Corgi. Reprinted by permission of The Random House Group Ltd; p. 230: 'A Touch of Class' from *The Complete Fawlty Towers*, written by John Cleese and Connie Booth; p. 247: From Constance Cox's adaption of 'Lord Arthur Savile's Crime' by Oscar Wilde, published by Samuel French Ltd, 1963; p. 261: 'The Alchemist' by Ben Johnson, edited by Brian Woolland, Cambridge Literature Series, 1995 © Cambridge University Press, reproduced with permission.

The publishers would like to thank the following for permission to reproduce photographs:

pp. 6, 188, 245: © BBC Photo Library; p. 24: Paramount/Everett Collection/Rex Features; pp. 29, 85, 122, 271: Photostage; p. 55 A scene from the 2005 performance of *Death and the King's Horseman* by the School of Music & Theatre Arts, Washington State University; p. 88: © Robbie Jack/Corbis; p. 113: Dana Rice and Shanna Allman in a scene from the 2007 performance of *Trifles* by the Stone Soup Theatre, Seattle, Washington. Photo by Erik Stuhaug; p. 135: Renaissance Films/BBC/Curzon Films/ The Kobal Collection; p. 151: Ben Molyneux Travel Photography/Alamy; p. 170: Box TV Ltd; p. 193: Scott Burkell, Iris Leiberman and Joe Aiello in the 2003 production of *The Foreigner* by Barn Theatre, Augusta, Michigan; p. 218: from a performance of *Soudné Sestry* at Divaldo v Dlouhé (Theatre on Dlouhá), Prague. Photo by Martin Špelda; p. 248: *Lord Arthur Savile's Crime* produced by Oxford Theatre Guild, December 2003. Photo by Bill Moulford